SPECTRAL STALKERS

The Aleph is a prize beyond all measure, a mysterious artefact from another dimension which can be used to harness all the forces of the Universe. Within the swirling globe one may gaze at an exact copy of all the planes of existence — or perhaps at existence itself!

Now, whether by fate or fortune, the Aleph has arrived in Khul and been entrusted to YOU for safekeeping. YOU must use its unearthly powers to transport you through the dimensions and overcome the many obstacles in your way until you can return it to its rightful owner. But beware, for others also seek to own the Aleph — especially the terrifying Spectral Stalkers!

Two dice, a pencil and an eraser are all you need to embark on this astonishing adventure, which is complete with its elaborate combat system and a score sheet to record your progress.

Many dangers lie ahead and your success is by no means certain. Powerful adversaries are ranged against you, and it's up to YOU to decide which route to follow, which dangers to risk and which foes to fight. Nothing has prepared you for an adventure like this!

Fighting Fantasy Gamebooks

Steve Jackson and Ian Livingstone

present

by **Peter Darvill-Evans**

Illustrated by Tony Hough

PUFFIN BOOKS

PUFFIN BOOKS

Published by the Penguin Group
Penguin Books Ltd, 27 Wrights Lane, London W8 5TZ, England
Penguin Books USA Inc., 375 Hudson Street, New York, New York 10014, USA
Penguin Books Australia Ltd, Ringwood, Victoria, Australia
Penguin Books Canada Ltd, 10 Alcorn Avenue, Toronto, Ontario, Canada M4V 3B2
Penguin Books (NZ) Ltd, 182–190 Wairau Road, Auckland 10, New Zealand

Penguin Books Ltd, Registered Offices: Harmondsworth, Middlesex, England

First published 1991
3 5 7 9 10 8 6 4 2

Printed in England by Clays Ltd, St Ives plc
Filmset in 12/13 Palatino

CONTENTS

All ye who would of symbols speak
With Semeion the Seer,
Through courtyard maze him ye must seek:
The paths are mirror'd here.

Pause for reflection; study ye
These twisting tracks of rock.
The winding ways reveal the key;
The gate ye must unlock.

Danger dwells in many squares;
Only a few are gainful.
Seek out the good, and shun the lairs
Where entry will be painful.

ADVENTURING AMONG THE SPHERES

You are a warrior, a hardy adventurer with remarkable skills. You will use dice to determine your exact attributes, and on pages 14–15 there is an *Adventure Sheet* on which you will record your scores and the incidents of your adventure. Use a pencil, or make photocopies of the *Adventure Sheet*, as you will almost certainly need to make more than one attempt to escape the relentless Spectral Stalkers and prevent the enslavement of the Universe.

Skill, Stamina and Luck

Roll one die. Add 6 to the score and enter the total in the SKILL box on the *Adventure Sheet*.

Roll two dice. Add 12 to the score and enter the total in the STAMINA box.

Roll one die. Add 6 to the score and enter the total in the LUCK box.

These are your *Initial* scores and you must keep a permanent record of them. All of your scores may change during your adventure, but they will exceed your *Initial* amounts only on very rare occasions. You must keep a record of all changes to your scores – so write small or use a rubber.

Your SKILL score reflects your expertise in combat, your ability with weapons and your dexterity. Your STAMINA is your health, fitness, and ability to survive wounds and physical hardship. Your LUCK score shows how lucky you are.

Combat

During your adventure you will meet other people and creatures. Some of them will attack you; others you will decide to fight. The procedure for resolving battles is described below.

SKILL and STAMINA scores are given in the text for each opponent that you meet. Write these scores in the first vacant Encounter Box on your *Adventure Sheet*. Record also any special abilities or instructions that are unique to this particular opponent. The sequence is then:

1. Roll two dice for your opponent. Add the total to his SKILL score. This is his Attack Strength.

2. Roll two dice and add the total to your current SKILL score. This is your Attack Strength.

3. If your Attack Strength is the higher, you have wounded your opponent. Go to step 4. If your opponent's Attack Strength is higher, he has wounded you. Go to step 5. If the Attack Strength totals are the same, you have avoided each other's blows – start a new Combat Round from step 1.

4. Subtract 2 points from your opponent's STAMINA.

You may be able to deduct additional points if you use your LUCK (see below) or if you have a special weapon.

5. Subtract 2 points from your STAMINA. You may use your LUCK here to reduce the amount you lose (see below).

6. Make sure you have recorded on the *Adventure Sheet* all adjustments to STAMINA and LUCK scores.

7. Begin the next Combat Round, starting again at step 1. This sequence continues until either you or your opponent has a STAMINA score of zero. If your opponent's STAMINA score reaches zero, you have killed him and can continue with your adventure. If your STAMINA score reaches zero, you are dead; you must start the adventure again from the beginning, having rolled dice to create a new character.

Often you will have to fight more than one opponent at the same time. Sometimes you will treat them as a single opponent; sometimes you will be able to fight them one at a time; and sometimes all of them will be able to attack you while you defend yourself and attack only one of them. Specific instructions will be given at the appropriate point whenever you meet more than one opponent.

Luck

There will be times when the success or failure of your exploits will depend entirely on your LUCK. You will be instructed to *Test your Luck*, the procedure for which is as follows: roll two dice. If the total score is equal to or less than your LUCK score, you are Lucky and the outcome will be in your favour. If the total is higher than your LUCK score, you are Unlucky. Whatever the outcome, you must deduct 1 point from your LUCK score. As you will see, the more you use your LUCK, the less likely you are to be Lucky. There will be occasions when you are able to recover some points of LUCK, but unless specifically stated your score cannot exceed its *Initial* value.

Using Luck in Combat

You can use your LUCK in combat to inflict a particularly serious wound, or to minimize a wound that has been inflicted on you.

Whenever you wound an opponent, you may *Test your Luck*: roll two dice; if the total score is equal to or less than your LUCK score, you have been Lucky. If the total is higher than your LUCK score, you are Unlucky. Whatever the result, you must deduct 1 point from your current LUCK score. If you are Lucky, you have inflicted a severe wound: deduct an *extra* 2 points from your opponent's STAMINA. If you are Unlucky, you have merely grazed him, and you deduct 1 *less* point of STAMINA than normal.

If you have been wounded, you can *Test your Luck* in exactly the same way. Remember to deduct 1 point from your LUCK whatever the result. If you are Lucky, the wound was only a glancing blow, and you can deduct 1 *less* point of STAMINA than usual. If you are Unlucky, the wound is serious: deduct 1 *extra* STAMINA point.

Restoring Skill and Stamina

Skill

Your SKILL will not change much during your adventure, and you should change it only if given specific instructions in the text. As SKILL is a measure of combat prowess, it can be reduced by losing your weapon or by the effects of poison, for instance; acquiring a magical weapon could increase your SKILL – but remember that you can use only one weapon at a time!

Stamina

Your STAMINA will change frequently during your adventure as you suffer wounds and then recover. At various times you will be given opportunities to eat meals and to acquire Provisions. Eating a meal normally restores up to 4 points of STAMINA, although there may be times, indicated in the text, when you get so hungry you will need to eat a meal simply to avoid losing STAMINA. You may eat only one meal at a time, even though you may have more in your backpack. Unless specifically stated, your STAMINA may never exceed its *Initial* score.

Leaving a Trail

Spectral Stalkers can detect the traces of psychic energy that you leave in your wake as you travel between the Spheres of the Macrocosmos. Each time that you pay more than a flying visit to a location – if you stay long enough to become involved in a fight, for instance –

you will leave a disturbance in the ether that will attract the Spectral Stalkers. The more times you do this, the easier it is for your shadowy pursuers to home in on you.

Your TRAIL score shows how easy it is for the Spectral Stalkers to find you. At the start of your adventure your TRAIL score is zero – the Spectral Stalkers do not even know of your existence, and have no chance of finding you. At various points in your adventure, however, you will be instructed to add TRAIL points to your score. Thus, the longer you spend on your travels, the greater the risk that the Spectral Stalkers will find you.

At other times you will be instructed to *Test your Trail Score*. The procedure for this is: roll three dice. If the total rolled is equal to or more than your TRAIL score, you remain undetected; if the total rolled is less than your TRAIL score, you have been detected by the Spectral Stalkers.

Often you will be told to add a point to your TRAIL score and then to *Test your Trail Score* immediately afterwards.

Getting Started

You start this adventure with no inkling of the heavy task that is about to fall to you, and no premonition that in the days to come you will be pursued by a pack of nightmarish creatures more inexorable than Bloodhounds and more vicious than Wolves. Instead, you are carefree: you have no employment and your backpack contains Provisions for only two more meals, but your purse is full and you have the world to go adventuring in. Your trusty sword is, as ever, at your side.

It is recommended that you make notes and draw a map as you explore. There is a way to succeed that involves little risk, even if you start with low *Initial* scores. There are many more routes that lead to failure and unpleasant fates.

Start with the *Background* section; then go on to the section headed with the number 1. After that go to whichever numbered section you are instructed to.

ADVENTURE SHEET

| SKILL *Initial Skill=* | STAMINA *Initial Stamina=* | LUCK *Initial Luck=* |

WEAPONS

TRAIL *Initial Trail=0*

POTIONS AND MAGICAL ITEMS

GOLD

OTHER OBJECTS AND EQUIPMENT

PROVISIONS REMAINING

ENCOUNTER BOXES

Skill= *Stamina=*	*Skill=* *Stamina=*	*Skill=* *Stamina=*
Skill= *Stamina=*	*Skill=* *Stamina=*	*Skill=* *Stamina=*
Skill= *Stamina=*	*Skill=* *Stamina=*	*Skill=* *Stamina=*
Skill= *Stamina=*	*Skill=* *Stamina=*	*Skill=* *Stamina=*

BACKGROUND

'Signs and portents,' wheezes the old fortune-teller in a voice that seems to rumble from within the folds of his moth-eaten cloak. 'There are signs and portents here. The cards will speak the truth for you, young warrior. I feel it.'

You are beginning to wish that you had never ventured into this dark and smelly tent. The raucous shrieks and music and laughter of the fairground sound dim and distant, even though the grubby canvas of the fortune-teller's tent is the only thing that separates you from the merry-making crowds. You could be outside in the sunshine enjoying the Midsummer Fair instead of waiting in half-darkness for this ancient half-Elven charlatan to start his card-reading act.

A gust of cold wind swirls around you without disturbing the smoke that clogs the air. Suddenly apprehensive, you shiver. The fortune-teller seems momentarily alarmed, but then clears his throat and begins to turn over the cards, one by one.

Each disc of thick parchment bears a faded picture. The first few are familiar – a shining gemstone, a tramp with his meagre belongings tied in a bundle, a skeleton wielding a scythe. The fortune-teller's explanation is equally ordinary – the usual patter about a great treasure and going on a long and difficult journey, and the threat of terrible danger. Since when did your life as an adventurer contain anything but treasure, travel and danger? You regret giving the old half-Elf a Gold Piece; you now have only 8 Gold Pieces left in your purse and there are many more stalls to visit before nightfall.

Then you notice that the fortune-teller has stopped mumbling. He is staring at the card he has just turned over. His hands are shaking. The face of the new card is completely blank and slightly luminous. At last he manages to stutter: 'It – it isn't possible! None of these cards is blank! But if this is so . . . This card represents your destination, soldier. I fear for you.'

'Why? What does it mean? Where is my destination?'

'Not in Khul,' wails the fortune-teller. 'Nor anywhere in this world. You will travel further than any man can imagine, with a perilous burden and a dreadful pursuit at your heels. Go from here. A storm approaches. Prepare yourself: you will be plucked from this world ere long.'

You step outside to find dark clouds racing across the sky. The crowds are dispersing and the fairground folk are struggling to secure their tents against a rising gale. The paths across the fields to Neuburg are thronged with townspeople scurrying home. You decide to shelter from the storm in the forest, and you set out alone towards the dark line of trees . . .

Turn to **1**.

1

You hurry towards the forest beneath the billowing black clouds that have turned daylight into dusk. There is a sudden flash of blinding light. You expect a crash of thunder, but instead there is an eerie silence. Then you see something falling out of the sky, tumbling and fluttering like an autumn leaf. It lands with a thump on the path ahead and you run towards it.

It is a winged creature unlike any that you have seen before, and it is badly hurt. Its silver, gossamer-thin wings and its bright robes have been torn into tattered shreds; its small humanoid body bears grievous wounds. It stirs as you approach, and stares at you with huge round eyes. With its last reserves of strength it holds out to you the bundle that it carries, and tries to speak: 'Stranger! I am dying . . . I have failed. Take this burden from me! Take it! Archmage Globus . . . he must . . . Too late! I am dying. Take it! . . . and beware the Spectral Stalkers! . . .'

The creature dies. You pick up the bundle. It seems to be a hard ball wrapped in a cloth. Will you put the bundle in your backpack and continue on your way (turn to **207**), or unwrap the cloth and look at its contents (turn to **316**)?

2

You pull the Aleph from your backpack, but you are appalled to see that, instead of containing an infinite array of glowing images, it is grey and cloudy. As you stare into the sphere, the shifting forms congeal into the indistinct likeness of a face — and a voice thrusts itself into your mind. 'Ah! So you are here!' gloats the voice. 'You have brought the prize to me. How considerate. Now you cannot escape!' Add 1 point to your TRAIL score. Hurriedly you stuff the Aleph back into your pack; it seems that your travels will end, one way or another, on this world. You decide to keep moving; will you walk towards the water (turn to **92**) or the plains (turn to **116**)?

3

You cannot hope to prevail against all the citizens of this city. You fight with all your strength, but this only increases the determination of the Elves to capture you alive for sacrifice to their deity Vacavon. It also increases your TRAIL score by 1 point. Eventually you are surrounded, subdued, and given several sharp kicks as a reward for causing so much trouble. Deduct 2 points of STAMINA, and turn to **301**.

4

Apart from a few Silica Serpents writhing in glittering coils high in the turquoise sky, you don't see a single creature during your long trek to the curtain of cliffs that supports the highest level of the Ziggurat World. The path becomes steeper and steeper until it is zig-zagging up the precipitous wall of rock – and finally it peters out altogether. You stop to rest. If you have Provisions, you can eat one meal and restore up to 4 points of STAMINA. Then you resume the ascent; from here onwards you will be rock-climbing. If you are wearing Ophidian armour, turn to **321**; if not, turn to **254**.

5

The Spectral Stalker has failed to find you. You heave a sigh of relief as the hideous creature shakes its great head in frustration and begins to dissolve into the air. Night is falling, and a cold wind is blowing across the wild countryside. There is nowhere except the inn to shelter for the night; if you decide to go in, turn to **222**. If you would rather use the Aleph to transport you elsewhere, turn to **283**.

6

The tinkling of the bell is lost in the oppressive silence. You wait but nothing happens. You are about to walk away when a figure rises behind the desk and huffs a cloud of smoke. You jump back in surprise and alarm; a female Dragon is glaring down at you over a pair of wire-framed spectacles.

'Yes? Well, what do you want? This is the Library in Limbo, you know, and no place for warriors and other troublemakers.'

Will you show the Dragon the sphere, and ask her what it is (turn to 395), or ask her if she has heard of Globus and the Spectral Stalkers (turn to 93)? Or will you attack her (turn to 340)?

7

You heave a sigh of relief as the Spectral Stalker dissolves into the air, but you have little time to reflect on your good fortune. The Black Shadows return, in greater numbers than ever. With no energy to resist their attack, you are soon overwhelmed, and you feel sharp fangs piercing your flesh. The venom works quickly and you drift into unconsciousness. Turn to 291.

8

You strike the harp from the Minstrel's hands. It continues to sing; but as the Minstrel turns to confront you, his face contorted with rage, the harp's melody falters. The Zwinians begin to recover their wits, but you have little time to notice them. Your attention is fixed on the sword-wielding Minstrel, whose appearance is changing even as he attacks you. His human appearance was an illusion: he is really Barogkaz, a large, powerfully-built Zwinian, and a formidable swordsman.

BAROGKAZ   SKILL 9   STAMINA 13

If you survive three rounds of combat, the citadel guards join the fray and quickly subdue Barogkaz. Frampa, Lord of the Citadel, is grateful for your help but is still suspicious of you. He orders you to take the Minstrel's harp and leave his domain. You find a secluded hollow outside the town walls and decide to abandon the harp there before using the Aleph. Then, to your surprise, the harp speaks: 'Do not forsake me, warrior, for I am no ordinary harp. I am the living spirit of the Minstrel Cerod, whose form the foul beast Barogkaz usurped. Even if you have no skill in music, I can help you.' The harp will halve the SKILL of any humanoid opponent you fight; but, because it will not fit inside your pack, you must reduce your SKILL by one point while you have it. If you decide to keep the harp, record it on your *Adventure Sheet*; whether or not you keep it, your next step is to use the Aleph – turn to **91**.

9

Necromon's eyes begin to glint with a manic light. 'You promised to help me,' he whispers. 'You gave your word. I need your life force. You must let me have it!' He advances on you, pulling a massive cleaver from the rack of knives beside his butcher's block. You try to retreat towards the door, but the white-coated madman lunges past you and blocks your escape. You decide to make for the other door — the one through which Necromon entered the room — but while you are backing towards it you will have to fight.

NECROMON   SKILL 7   STAMINA 6

This should be an easy fight to win, particularly as Necromon seems not to be concentrating on using his cleaver; but than is because he is concentrating on *you*. After each Attack Round, roll two dice; if the total is greater than your SKILL, you find your eyes inexplicably drawn to his — and you are suddenly convinced that you should agree to whatever he asks you to do. Turn to **249**. If you evade his gaze, and survive the fight, you find that after two rounds of combat you can retreat through the door. As you do so, Necromon's cleaver gashes your shoulder — deduct 2 points of STAMINA, and, if you are still alive, turn to **366**.

10

The clouds part; sunlight floods the field. Drawenna's laughter fills the sky. 'That's it!' she shouts. 'That, my brave pawn, my clever pawn, is exactly the right move. Hold! Do not attack. Burud! Do you see the position? My three warriors are in a triangle — and three of yours are at their mercy. Victory is mine. Concede, and I'll spare your wretched pawns.'

'What do I care for mere pawns?' Burud's voice is choked with anger. 'Kill them or not, as you see fit. I won't remain to watch. I'll find other ways to get you, Drawenna!' A gale swirls the clouds across the sky and

into the distance. You find that you can release your hold on the pike; the metal armour slips from your back. With the other surviving warriors you wander to the edge of the field, where you find your backpack, your clothes, and a purse containing 10 Gold Pieces (note this on your *Adventure Sheet*).

Drawenna's voice addresses you again. 'I would ask you to stay, brave warrior,' she says, 'but I sense you are on a perilous quest and cannot linger. Take this!' A golden ring falls out of the sky and lands at your feet; you pick it up and marvel at the large blue gemstone set into it. 'The jewel is not only decorative,' says Drawenna's voice. 'If you are weary, or sorely wounded, swallow the blue gem. It will restore your strength.' You can use this item at any time, but only once; swallowing the gem will restore up to 6 points of STAMINA. Record it on your *Adventure Sheet*. Drawenna is right: you have to move on. Turn to **124**.

11

You step into a square room with walls lined with sagging bookshelves. Precarious piles of books also cover the floor and several tables. Seated at a desk is a small humanoid in grey robes; two others are frantically examining one of the piles of books and writing notes on parchment scrolls. As you enter they all stop working and stare at you. The seated one squeaks at you: 'Are you Admittance?'

'No,' you reply. 'Of course not.'

'Well come in, then, and we'll classify you.' You

approach his desk, and ask him what he and his companions are doing. 'We are Ranganathans,' he announces. 'And we're classifying, of course. The question is: what are you?' You say you are a human, and a warrior. 'Well, which is it? Human or Warrior? You can't be two things at once. You're obviously a difficult case. And what do we do with difficult cases, boys?'

'Take them to pieces! That's the way to find out!' chorus the other two Ranganathans, creeping towards you and flexing their sharp fingers. Will you fight them off (turn to **328**), or look for a way out (turn to **74**)?

You begin the ascent of the cliff, doggedly trudging up the rocky path that winds back and forth across the sheer face. Eventually, you have to pause to rest. Looking down, you are almost overcome with vertigo when you see how small and distant the landscape below you has become. Looking upward, you see that you are only a little more that half-way up the cliff-face. You shrink against the rocks as a couple of glittering Silica Serpents swoop past, then continue climbing, passing through a layer of white clouds that leave droplets of cold water all over you, before reaching a ledge where you take another rest. If you have Provisions, you can eat one meal and restore up to 4 points of STAMINA. Two paths lead upwards from the ledge: one, to your right as you face the cliff, zig-zags towards a craggy part of the clifftop that is dotted with tall cylindrical towers; the other climbs slowly to a distant and relatively flat part of the clifftop. Will you take the path to the right (turn to **130**), or the left (turn to **146**)?

turn to **130**), or the left (turn to **146**)?

13

As you run down the avenue you can hear the Golem pounding after you, each stride shaking the ground. With angry swipes of its mallet the monster destroys the clay statues as it passes them. The Golem is catching up with you; you veer off the path and on to the bare hillside, hoping that as the hot sun dries the monster's body it will begin to slow down. But now the Golem is right behind you, its mallet smashing boulders to your right and left as you dodge the blows.

Roll one die. The result is the number of times that you have to dodge the mallet-blows. For each dodge, roll two dice; each time that the result is higher than your SKILL you are struck by shards of rock and must deduct 2 points of STAMINA. However, because the Golem is at last beginning to slow, you may deduct one point from the second dice-roll, two from the third, three from the fourth, and so on. If you survive the mallet-blows, you are rewarded by the sight of the Golem slowing down as the sun's rays dry its body. After a few minutes, it is completely motionless: a clay statue that will remain lifeless on the hillside until the next rainstorm. You make your way back to the cave in the cliff-face; turn to **263**.

14

The descent is difficult, and by the time you reach the base of the tower nearly every one of your little group of ex-prisoners has almost slipped from the narrow stairway at least once. Now, huddled in the darkness at the bottom of the ravine, you discuss your next move. All of the Elves, Vaskind and Mantirs want to return to their homes, and that entails taking the long zig-zag path down the cliff to the lower level of the Ziggurat World. You agree to accompany them to the top of the cliff. Turn to 333.

15

You walk for some distance along a roughly-hewn tunnel, and then, after stooping under an arch, you find that the tunnel divides. You are standing between three doorways; in the dim light you can see that only one of them has the circle and triangle symbol carved into its lintel. You face this doorway and, looking through it, you can see daylight at the end of a long tunnel; the other two tunnels, with unmarked doorways, are to your right and left. Will you go straight on, towards the daylight (turn to 305); to your right (turn to 367); or to your left (turn to 206)?

16

You are too slow. The Tyrant plucks the Aleph from your fingers and immediately begins to disappear into it. You can only watch in horror as the sphere expands, and then contracts to a point – and disappears. You have lost the Aleph. You are stranded on this barren world where, year after year, the dwindling Feliti bring offerings to your castle and perform half-forgotten rituals in their overgrown garden. You are the new Tyrant. Perhaps, after a few centuries, a new Champion will appear on the stone table in the Feliti garden . . .

17

Although there is no sound – even the flowers have stopped tinkling throughout the Crystal Garden – you can hear the Spectral Stalker's scream of rage reverberate inside your mind as it dissolves into the air. It knew that it had almost found you, and you know it too. You step over the Silica Serpent and hurry towards the Vitreous Citadel. Turn to **336**.

18

Grondel convinces the priest that you have proof of the existence of other worlds. The two Elves watch in fascination as you unwrap the glowing sphere and reveal its vista of multitudinous lands and planets. Grondel stares open-mouthed in amazement; the priest reels backwards, overwhelmed by this shock to the foundations of his beliefs. You cover the Aleph and pack it away, but a little damage has already been done – add 1 point to your TRAIL score. Grondel promises to reward you for your help, and he leads you to his house. As you eat the meal he provides for you – it has almost no taste, but it restores up to 4 points of STAMINA – Grondel rummages in chests and cupboards until he finds a silver ring with a small stone in a cumbersome setting. 'This is not the most attractive of jewels,' he chuckles, 'but it is very useful. If you twist the setting – like this – the Ring of Light will provide illumination. Such items are valuable here in the darkness, but I hope that you will find it of some worth in your travels.' You assure Grondel that the ring will indeed be very useful, and you slip it on to a finger. The old Elf starts to busy himself with plans for an expedition to leave the cave and you take your leave. Turn to 377.

19

Your pulse pounds in your head as the water crushes you. A trickle of precious air escapes from your clenched lips as you fight to remain conscious, your body rising slowly through the icy waters. Roll four dice; if the total is less than your current STAMINA, turn to 194; if the total is equal to, or greater than, your STAMINA, turn to **84**.

There is nothing else of interest in the courtyard and you consider which of its four doorways you will leave through. There is a portal in each of the four walls; you turn to face the doorway which has the circle and triangle symbol carved above it. Which way will you go:

Through the door you are facing?	Turn to **257**
The door behind you?	Turn to **329**
The door to your right?	Turn to **335**
The door to your left?	Turn to **78**

21

You are in an unlit tunnel. You can see nothing, and can feel only the cool, smooth stones on both sides. You grope towards the indistinct sound of chanting voices. The chanting becomes louder, urgent and frenzied. You take one more step, the floor gives way beneath your feet, and you are sliding helplessly down a chute and into flickering light. You land on a dais of rune-carved flagstones and, as you pick yourself up, you see that you have emerged from the mouth of a gigantic stone skull that forms one wall of the torchlit hall. The voices are suddenly silent. You turn to find yourself looking up into the fiery eye-sockets of another skull – but this one is the living face of a giant warrior-priest, who howls with joy as he thanks his grim deity.

'As I foretold, mighty Glund, you have given us an omen. This creature will be our victory sacrifice. I, Syzuk the Devastator, will shed its lifeblood at the battle's end on an altar of a thousand vanquished foes. Warriors! Can you now doubt our victory? To arms!'

Two soldiers begin to climb on to the platform. Will you fight them (turn to **139**), wait for them to capture you (turn to **85**), or try to escape by re-entering the mouth of the stone skull (turn to **348**)?

22

By the time you reach the foot of the rock face, the Ophidians are already little more than black dots in the distance and their captive Silica Serpent is a shimmering sliver of light hanging in the air beside them. You are relieved to find that the surface of the rock is not as smooth as it first appeared: there are crevices and outcrops for your feet and hands. You begin the long ascent, pulling yourself upwards centimetre by precarious and painful centimetre. This climb will test both your strength and your endurance. Roll six dice. If the total is equal to, or less than, the sum of your SKILL and STAMINA, turn to **218**; if the total is greater than the sum of your SKILL and STAMINA, turn to **86**.

23

As Semeion leads you back to his courtyard gardens he gives you some last words of advice. 'Go to the Ziggurat World of the Archmage Globus,' he says thoughtfully. 'Whether danger or good fortune await you there, the Ziggurat World is the place where your travelling must end. The Aleph will take you there. Be on your guard at all times.' You thank the old man, and ask him if he can provide you with more substantial assistance — food, for instance. Semeion shakes his head. 'I do not require sustenance such as your body needs,' he says, 'for this shape in which you see me is but one of many forms. From my storehouse of wisdom, however, I offer these two further thoughts: catch the fisher in his own nets; and set the hunter's hounds upon the hunter.' You manage to sound grateful for these homilies as you take the Aleph from your backpack. If you have no weapon you can ask Semeion if he can provide one — turn to **182**; otherwise, you lose yourself in the Aleph's swarming worlds — turn to **234**.

24

The cramped cabin at the back of the wagon is full of magician's props and theatrical costumes, jumbled boxes and crates – and, imprisoned in a cage suspended from the ceiling, a young woman who must be the Baron's missing daughter. You hear the crack of a whip and the whinnying of horses, and with a jolt the wagon begins to move, accelerating rapidly over the cobblestones as the Conjuror and his assistant make good their escape from the town. You unstrap your backpack and search for something to help you force open the cage's sturdy lock, but without success. 'The Conjuror has the key,' the Baron's daughter says in an excited voice, 'and I expect he'll come soon to check that I'm still a prisoner!' You fear she is correct. Will you wait for the Conjuror's entrance (turn to 137), or use the Aleph to transport you away from this place (turn to 63)?

25

'Why do you hesitate?' the Archmage demands, his voice growing dark and cold. 'Do you dare to defy me? You do not know the extent of my powers. I have servants, demons from beyond this plane of existence, who will destroy you. The Spectral Stalkers will come at my bidding. Give me the Aleph – or prepare to die!' You have no doubt that you would be powerless against the otherworldly might of the Spectral Stalkers. If you decide that you have no choice but to hand the Aleph to Globus, turn to 338; if you insist on keeping it, turn to 172.

26

After walking in the darkness of the tunnel for some time, you grope your way round a corner and see light beyond a doorway ahead. Ducking through the stone portal you find yourself in a small, square chamber with a doorway set in each of the four walls. A shaft of brilliant sunlight streams from high above on to a glowing boulder set into the tiled floor. The boulder emanates a fierce heat and within seconds you find the temperature unbearable. You decide to leave quickly, but you have time to read the words which are carved above the doorways:

> *Symbols can reveal that which has been*
> *And that which is.*
> *Only you know what you intend.*
> *No man knows what will happen.*

You face the circle and triangle symbol, and must choose which doorway you will leave through:

The door you are facing?	Turn to **224**
The door behind you?	Turn to **101**
The door to your left?	Turn to **367**
The door to your right?	Turn to **187**

27

You turn and stare in surprise. In front of you there is a doorway which you are sure was not there a minute ago. It looks solid enough; on its stone lintel is engraved the word *EXIT*. It seems that you have found the way out – or perhaps it has found you! Anything would be better than these endless corridors, you decide, and walk into the black shadow in the doorway. Turn to **185**.

28

You press yourself against the wall while you reach for the silver dagger, feeling drops of the Black Shadow's foul-smelling venom fall on to your shoulders. When the monster's fangs are only centimetres above your head you thrust the dagger upwards. Although your blow misses its target, the Black Shadow hisses in alarm and tries to scuttle backwards. You thrust a second time and the creature screeches as it loses its grip on the stones and flutters downwards like a torn rag in a gust of wind. Restore 1 point of LUCK. Treading as quickly as you dare, you continue up the crumbling steps. Turn to **318**.

29

You breathe a sigh of relief as the awful shape dissolves into the air. Add 1 point to your TRAIL score. You look about you. The landscape of woodland and meadows is dominated by a wall of impossibly tall, sheer cliffs that extend across half the horizon, and thin, cylindrical towers dot the crags atop the cliffs. In the hazy distance, far beyond and above the clifftops, you can just make out an even higher flat-topped mountain. Beyond a few floating fluffy clouds, and a few winged creatures that swoop amongst them, the sky is sharply divided into two parts: an area of absolute darkness and a turquoise area that glows with golden light. There is no sun. You are on the Ziggurat World, a planet of terraces enclosed within a half-dark, half-light sphere. You hear the sound of approaching voices and recognize the lilting note of a Wood Elf dialect. Will you wait to see who is coming (turn to 370), or walk towards the cliffs and take advantage of the rising land to gain an overview of this level of the world (turn to 190)?

30

You take the Aleph from your backpack and hold it in your hands. The countless vistas that swarm within the shining sphere, tiny yet perfect in every detail, entrance you immediately. Strange creatures, alien peoples, towns, continents, planets, swirling stars and cloudy galaxies swim before your eyes. You feel yourself being enveloped by the Aleph, and transported within it. Roll one die. If you roll an even number, turn to 135; if you roll an odd number, turn to 145.

31

The doorway says nothing more, but after a moment of ominous calm, the stone slab suddenly starts to vibrate furiously, while at the same time lashing from side to side and rocking up and down. You realize that you will be shaken from the bridge and into the moat within seconds: your only hope is to jump to safety.

Will you try to leap back to the bank (turn to **279**), or forwards, into the mouth of the doorway (turn to **311**)?

32
Now it is the turn of Burud's black warriors. They do not even bother to consult each other: you hear a noise and turn to see the black pawn on *E3* move to *F3*. You are caught between two black warriors and no matter how much you turn and turn again, your armour cannot protect you against attack from two opposite sides. You lose the game.

33
The silence does not last. You hear the sound of many feet coming through the grass. At first you fear a stampede of Colepods, but the strange beings that canter through the grass to surround you are Mantirs, the owners and shepherds of the Colepod herds. Like a Colepod, a Mantir resembles a giant insect, with a shell-like carapace and antennae waving from his forehead; but he walks upright, on only four legs, his foremost pair of limbs serving as arms. Each Mantir carries a spear and wears headgear as protection from the heat that beats upon the shadeless plains, and each has fashioned the knob of bone at the end of his tail into a spiked weapon of devastating effect. The Mantir herdsmen are as astounded by your appearance as they are grateful for the safe recovery of their rogue Colepod. Their leader silences their endless twittering comments and presents you with a reward — a large slice of delicious honeycake which can restore up to 4 STAMINA points. He then addresses you, speaking in a fluting

voice that you can barely understand. He asks what you are doing here on the plains; and, more importantly, whether you are a friend or an enemy of Globus the Archmage who, says the Mantir, is the ruler of all the peoples on this world. Will you say that you are Globus's friend (turn to **266**), or his enemy (turn to **304**)?

34

You have no time to select any special item from your backpack; you must fight with the weapon you have at hand. The figures advance, making no attempt to avoid your blows — and you realize quickly that your attack is having no effect. The man and the woman are as insubstantial as ghosts, but it seems they can harm you: any weapon you are using becomes too cold to hold on to, and you are obliged to drop it — delete it from your *Adventure Sheet* and reduce your SKILL by 2 points until you find another weapon. If you are attacking with your bare hands, your fist suffers frostbite as it passes through the apparitions — lose 3 points from your STAMINA. You turn and run. Turn to **262**.

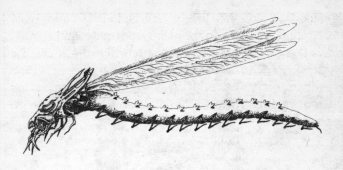

35

The Ophidians are momentarily confused: they can see that their comrade has fallen and that you are now unguarded, but they are reluctant to abandon the Silica Serpent before it has been completely secured. In this moment of uncertainty you make your escape. Leaping from boulder to boulder you make for the high ground above the gully in which the Ophidians trapped the Serpent. You take a last look down into the ravine, and note with satisfaction that the Ophidians have not set off in pursuit. You make for the vast cliffs in the distance. Turn to 4.

36

The Aleph's floating images condense into the glowing sphere that you hold cupped in your hands. You replace it in your backpack and look up. You are standing on a weathered stone table in the middle of an overgrown garden. You know at once that you are not on your home world of Titan: the sky shimmers like purple velvet, and floating in it are a vast pale sun and clouds like goose-down. The garden's plants are like rambling roses, but with dark leaves and aromatic magenta blooms; they have invaded the lawns, climbed the crumbling walls and embraced the carved figures of fabulous beasts that sit scowling on pedestals. There is a gate of wrought iron set into the wall and through it you see sharp-peaked mountains and a grim fortress. The gate opens; a procession enters the garden. The people are humanoid: small, with pale green skin, and green hair that rises in stiff spiral curls. They are wearing torn and dirty rags, but their leader has a fur-trimmed robe. With heads lowered they approach the stone table, and the leader begins a solemn prayer for the return of his people's champion. At the end of the incantation, he looks up – and his jaw drops in astonishment as he sees you. Will you greet these people (turn to **251**), or jump from the table and run out of the garden (turn to **323**)?

37

You hack away the remains of the net and scoop the feebly-protesting being into your arms. He is very light and you run quickly into the cover of the trees. No Wood Elves or Silica Serpents see you: restore 1 point of LUCK. 'You are as brave as you are foolhardy,' says the wounded creature as you lay him carefully on soft grasses, 'but I thank you once again. Had I been taken by the Silica Serpents I would have had to leave this body and I have many tasks to perform while I inhabit it. I see you are curious about me. I am a Mercurial, one of many messengers of — well, of those who guard the ways between the many worlds of the Macrocosmos. You have the Aleph, I know. And you must leave this place immediately! You have walked into a trap: this world is the home of Globus the Archmage. Globus has been consumed by his desire for knowledge and power. He is all evil now and will stop at nothing to acquire the Aleph. Flee before the Silica Serpents arrive to search for me, and flee from this world before Globus learns that you are here.' Spurred on by the Mercurial's words, you leave the trees and head towards the towering cliffs. Turn to 190.

You sit on the bed. As the light fades, the open doors of the toy cupboards seem dark and threatening, like the gaping mouths of monsters or the cave lairs of ferocious beasts. The rocking-horse appears to be watching you with its glass eye; the stuffed bear looks a little too realistic. Hanging on a hook is a jester's outfit that looks too large for a child; a goblin mask leers down at you from a shelf; an almost life-size ballerina doll has a smirk on her face; the little metal soldiers are holding sharp-pointed spears. On a table next to the bed a jointed clown doll sits inside a small glass sphere that seems to rock gently from side to side. Your feeling of relief is replaced by a sense of foreboding. If you have a

Glowcandle or a Ring of Light, turn to **87**; if not, turn
to **241**.

39

You start to move cautiously towards the door at the
other end of the room, but the monster shuffles sideways to block your path, holding out its various limbs
as if demanding something from you. The sheer size of
the creature deters you from attacking it; you have the
impression that even if you succeeded in hacking off
whole sections of its motley body it would scarcely
notice the loss. You will have to make a dash for the
door and hope that the monster's flailing limbs fail to
strike you. Roll a die and add the result to your SKILL;
then roll three dice for the monster. If the monster's
total is higher than yours, the difference is the number
of points of STAMINA you lose as an assortment of fists
and claws batter and tear you during your lunge towards the door. If you survive this onslaught you
succeed in reaching the door and slamming it behind
you. Turn to **258**.

40

In the morning you throw open the shutters of your
room. The wind seems even colder now, carrying with
it flurries of sleet and hail. You collect your belongings
and wander downstairs. The inn is deserted. You search
the cupboards and cellars, and find a sword that seems
sharp and well-balanced. You can keep it if you need a
weapon. It is not until you are about to leave the inn
that you find the most interesting item: pinned to the
back of the door is the innkeeper's licence, granted by

the Margrave of Neuburg – and dated four hundred years after the date when you found the Aleph.

Shaking your head in disbelief, you step out into the freezing rain. The door slams behind you and, shaken from its bracket, the inn sign falls from the outside wall and barely misses your head. You jump backwards and look down at the crude painting of two ghostly figures. The sign is circular, which seems unusual for an inn sign and uncannily reminiscent of the shape of the Aleph. It is small enough to fit into your backpack; perhaps you should pick it up and take it with you (record it on your *Adventure Sheet* if you do so). Khul, four hundred years in your future, seems an unwelcoming place. You bid it farewell and use the Aleph to go elsewhere. Turn to **283**.

41

The sound of the Colepod's pounding hooves fades into the distance, but the silence does not last. You hear the sound of many feet coming through the grass. At first you fear a stampede of Colepods, but the strange beings that canter through the grass to surround you are Mantirs, the owners and shepherds of the Colepod herds. Like a Colepod, a Mantir resembles a giant insect, with a shell-like carapace and antennae waving from his forehead; but he walks upright, on only four legs, his foremost pair of limbs serving as arms. Every Mantir carries a spear and each has fashioned the knob of bone at the end of his tail into a spiked weapon of devastating effect. The Mantir herdsmen are so astounded by your appearance that they forget all about their rogue Colepod. Their leader silences their endless twittering comments and addresses you in a fluting voice that you can barely understand. He asks what you are doing here on the plains and, more importantly, whether you are a friend or an enemy of Globus the Archmage who, he says, is the ruler of all the peoples on this world. Will you say you are Globus's friend (turn to 88), or his enemy (turn to 304)?

42

As soon as you step into the chamber at the heart of the machine, the rods that surround you begin to pulse with light and the room begins to fade. Then the pulsing lights themselves grow dim and, although your limbs are stationary and there is no sensation of speed, you feel yourself being transported to another place. Roll one die; if you roll:

1 or 2	Turn to 156
3 or 4	Turn to 354
5 or 6	Turn to 234

43

After only a few steps along the tunnel, you turn a corner and stumble down a flight of steep stairs. You fall into a vast cavern illuminated by bonfires and full of tethered Silica Serpents. Each Serpent is guarded by several Ophidians and within seconds you are surrounded by a dozen of the black-armoured beings. You cannot hope to fight your way out so you surrender. The Ophidians produce several lengths of strong rope and bind your limbs securely. Turn to 53.

44

You run beneath the canopy of branches, push through the undergrowth and throw yourself into a leafy dell. When you lift your head cautiously above the edge of the hollow and look back towards the path, you see that the monstrous shape has solidified and that a second is beginning to condense out of the air beside it. You watch with horrified fascination. These monsters must be the Spectral Stalkers that the winged creature spoke of; they are more hideous than the worst creations of your most sinister dreams. Each has four long, spindly legs, like those of a spider; a body that is no more than scaly skin drawn over sharp bones; a multitude of claw-tipped arms; and, for a head, a mass of writhing tentacles surmounted by two bulbous, faceted eyes like those of insects. You cannot hope to defeat them in combat and you dare not move, for fear that they will see you. You slide back to the bottom of the dell – and remember the bundle that the winged creature entrusted to you. Turn to 316.

45

You turn to face the doorway which has a triangle surmounted by a circle engraved on its lintel. Through which of the doorways will you leave this room:

The door in front of you?	Turn to 122
The door behind you?	Turn to 224
The door to your right?	Turn to 187
The door to your left?	Turn to 247

46

The first blaring note is enough to terrify the creatures that were about to attack you, scattering them like leaves in a gust of wind. Although you have exhausted the breath in your lungs, the noise from the Horn continues, becoming even louder, its strident note spreading across the barren landscape like a ripple across a pond. With your hands pressed to your ears to shut out the din, you see swarms of Black Shadows issuing from towers in frantic confusion. At last the Horn's blast fades. There are no Black Shadows to be seen – regain 1 point of LUCK. You run from the tower and scramble into the safety and darkness of the ravines. Turn to **214**.

47

The curtain is pulled aside and the Conjuror rushes past you, grabbing the Were-cat and pulling her along behind him. You join the crowd chasing the Conjuror along the passage and on to the front platform of the wagon, from which he and his assistant leap to the cobbles of the town square. You watch as they make off among the old houses of the town, pursued by the more enthusiastic elements of the crowd. The Baron's daughter is found locked in a cage suspended from the ceiling of the cabin at the back of the wagon, and is quickly freed. The Baron, grateful for your intervention, thrusts a purse into your hands: add 5 Gold Pieces to your *Adventure Sheet*. When you leave the wagon, however, you find that the townspeople are scattering in terror – your exertions in fighting the Were-cat have attracted the attention of your demonic pursuers. The hideous shape of a Spectral Stalker is forming in the air above the town square! Add 1 point to your TRAIL score. There seems to be no choice but to use the Aleph to leave this place. Turn to **63**.

48

The thick folds of fungus are much less solid than they looked, and your sword slices through them with ease. You hack energetically at the repellent stuff and the door is soon uncovered. In your haste, you fail to notice the clouds of tiny spores that are released from the fungus by your frenzied attack and you have no idea that the spores have landed all over your body until your skin starts to itch maddeningly. You must reduce your SKILL by 1 point because of the distraction caused by this irritation. Scratching yourself, you pull open the door, step through it, close it behind you and set off along the passage beyond. Turn to **148**.

49

Metron places the clay ball on a workbench. For many minutes the Mapmaker is busy with rulers, protractors, tubes of coloured fluids, and instruments with flashing lights and glowing numbers. Then he consults books from his library, draws a diagram of the ball and writes pages of notes. 'This is not a very interesting object,' Metron says at last. 'It is a hollow spheroid made from a mixture of substances that one might find in ordinary soil – full of impurities. It has been manufactured very inexactly: the diameter varies by as much as three sixty-fourths of a *dronk*. It cannot possibly serve any useful function. Shall I dispose of it for you?' You hurriedly pick up the clay ball; when you shake it, it no longer rattles. Metron has somehow removed the magic that Mayrek the Potter gave to the ball (note this on your *Adventure Sheet*). The ball still resembles the Aleph, however, and you decide to keep it. You complain bitterly to the Mapmaker that he has destroyed a magical item. Turn to 375.

50

You begin to despair of defeating the Silica Serpent. Add 1 point to your TRAIL score. You disengage from the struggle and see that the Elves are returning and more Silica Serpents are wheeling down from the skies. You realize that you cannot hope to defeat this many opponents and take to your heels. Under cover of the trees, you turn to see that you are not being pursued: the Elves and the Serpents are concerned only with the captive in the net. You make your way towards the towering cliffs – turn to 190.

51

You have arrived home – the continent of Khul. The trees, the landscape, the very air is familiar. You recognize the countryside: you are standing on a road along which you have marched many times. But everything has changed. The fields are a wilderness of heath and bracken, farm buildings ruined and almost smothered under brambles. The road has deteriorated into a muddy, rutted track. You walk along it until you can see the bridge over the River Gibelvatter – but the bridge is broken, and only a stump of stonework remains perched above the flowing waters. On this outcrop stands a new building, grim and battlemented. However, you see a circular inn sign swinging from a bracket on the wall and lights flicker behind the arrowslits in the upper storey. A heavily-built man is standing outside the only door; as you approach he draws his sword. Will you prepare to fight him (turn to **278**), or will you raise your open hands in a gesture of peace (turn to **319**)?

52

As the Feliti leader finishes his incantation, the heap of soft petals begins to glow. 'Now we must wait until night,' he says, 'and then I will explain our plight. If I may say so, Lord, you look weary. May we refresh you?' Without waiting for your reply, he orders several of the Feliti to bring you sweetmeats and wine. You taste the food: it seems wholesome. 'We will leave you now, Lord,' says the robed Feliti, 'and I will return after dark to speak with you. Have no fear. The eyes of the Tyrant cannot penetrate the thickets of the Eternal

Garden.' You decide to follow this advice and concentrate on eating (restore up to 4 points of STAMINA). When you look up from your meal, the sky is darkening – and in the place where there was a heap of flowers there is now only a glittering gem. The Jewel of Sleep has been created. You pick it up and see that it is a hollow crystal containing a purple liquid. If you want to take it and then use the Aleph to travel away from this world, note the Jewel on your *Adventure Sheet* and turn to **365**. If you wait in the garden, turn to **334**.

53

The Ophidians dump you on the floor of the cavern between two Silica Serpents who are as tightly bound as you are. Each has a chain round its neck which leads to an iron ring set into the cave wall, its wings held against its sinuous body by straps of leather and a muzzle enclosing most of its huge, scaly head. You endure the discomfort of your ropes as patiently as you can, and at last the Ophidians cease to watch over you and instead congregate at the far end of the cavern. As you are now unguarded, and near the entrance of the cavern, you think you could creep away undetected – if only you could break free of your bonds. You notice that the muzzles of the Silica Serpents are designed to avoid the creatures' corrosive venom – with the result that drops of it fall freely from the Serpents' jaws and burn hollows in the stone floor of the cavern. You wriggle across the rocks until you are lying beneath one of the Serpents' heads. Drops of venom fall on to your body; the liquid burns through the ropes, but it also burns you! Lose 3 points of STAMINA. If you survive, you can shrug off your bonds; and, taking with you a long coil of rope, you creep from the cavern. At the cave mouth, you have a choice: will you explore the right-hand tunnel (turn to 152), or will you use the rope to help you climb down to the foot of the rock wall and then continue towards the vast cliffs in the distance (turn to 4)?

54

Roll three dice and deduct the total from your STAM-INA. If, by some miracle, you are still alive, you regain your senses, groaning, your body racked with pain. You have survived the onslaught of the Spectral Stalkers — but where have they taken you? Turn to 392.

55

The Grappler's limbs hang limply at its sides; the lights in its transparent dome flash more slowly, then fade. As the last light dies, the all-pervasive hum suddenly ceases, the room lurches drunkenly — and in the huge hall of cages every door flies open, releasing the menagerie of bizarre life-forms. Soon hundreds of indescribable creatures are milling together in the hall; some are fighting, others are hunting or fleeing from predators, and all are creating a cacophony of discordant cries. Some of the fiercest-looking animals see you in the Transporter Bay and begin to prowl towards you; then, inexplicably, they turn tail and flee. You look behind you: the hideous shape of a Spectral Stalker is forming in the air! Add 1 point to your TRAIL score. You decide to use the Aleph to escape from this place and, feverishly, you pull the glowing sphere from your backpack and cup it in your hands. You feel yourself being enveloped by the Aleph, and transported within it. Roll one die. If you roll an even number, turn to **105**; if you roll an odd number, turn to **126**.

56

Something is moving inside your backpack. You nudge it with your foot: the glass ball is rocking from side to side – and inside it the little clown puppet is jumping up and down and hammering against the glass with his tiny fists. You stretch your leg and extricate the ball with your foot; then, with one swift blow of your booted heel, you shatter the glass. With the jerky movements of a marionette the little clown dances for joy before stooping to pick up a sliver of glass. He clambers laboriously up your clothing and along your arm, where he starts to slice through the ropes securing you to the pillar. As the last strands fall away from your body, the little puppet begins to change – and lying at your feet is the frail figure of a wizened old man. 'At last,' he wheezes with a smile. 'I have rescued a hero, and thus atoned for my dreadful deeds all those centuries ago. The curse is lifted from me, and at last I can die in peace!' With that, the old man expires. Delete the clown puppet from your *Adventure Sheet*. You look up to see the other prisoners staring at you in amazement. Turn to **296**.

57

The Minstrel and his harp remain silent as you accompany them along the road, which winds through the forest and eventually begins to rise into rockier terrain. At last you reach the summit as the road passes through a neck between two crags and you stop alongside the Minstrel to survey the wooded plateau in front of you. In the distance there is a walled citadel, its granite keep dominating the highest point. Two more Zwinian soldiers emerge from a small watchtower near the road. The Minstrel thumps the harp slung across his back and the instrument starts to sing. Enthralled by the eerie melody, the Zwinian guards seem befuddled and clumsy. The Minstrel draws his sword and runs at them, and in the ensuing mêlée succeeds in killing both of them. 'It is so sweet to dispose of these traitors,' he says, wiping his sword on a clump of grass, 'and this is but the beginning of my revenge. Shall we continue to the citadel? I promise you a wealth of entertainment there.' If you find the Minstrel's attitude too bloodthirsty you can decline his offer and walk away – turn to 342. If you decide to accompany him to the citadel, turn to 213.

58

The liquid is tasteless and you have gulped down several mouthfuls before you start to feel sharp pains in your stomach. You have swallowed embalming fluid, a poisonous substance used for preserving dead bodies! You writhe on the floor, retching helplessly. Deduct 3 points of STAMINA. If you survive the effects of the poison, the pain subsides and you recover gradually, until you feel strong enough to totter up the stairs and through the door. Turn to 189.

59

'Ill-mannered lout!' roars Wayland as you rush towards
him. 'Can't you take a joke? Be off with you!' You
suddenly notice that a doorway has appeared between
you and your opponent. The stone pillars look solid
and permanent, but you are sure it was not there a
moment ago. Through the doorway you see Wayland
grinning at you, and as you step under the lintel you
catch sight of the word *EXIT* engraved in the stone.
Turn to **185**.

60

You heave a sigh of relief as the Spectral Stalker dissolves into the air; it had almost found you and you could feel the tendrils of its malevolent will licking at the edges of your mind. The Vaskind have all fled beneath the waves; you are alone on the beach. You wander back and forth, but can find nothing of interest, and you decide to climb the path that zig-zags up the face of the cliff. Turn to 12.

61

You pull the glowing sphere from your backpack and gaze into it. The endless vista of numberless worlds spreads itself before you; wherever you look new marvels unfold before your eyes. The Aleph seems to be everywhere, surrounding you, carrying you away among the swirling spheres; with an effort you try to concentrate on your destination. If you are hoping to find someone who can explain the significance of the objects you have collected in your travels, turn to 354; if you are keen to reach the conclusion of your quest, turn to 234.

62

You charge into the midst of the glass flowers, striking to the right and left of you as you run. The air is filled with the noise of splintering glass and the wailing shrieks released by the flowers as they are cut down. On all sides of you there are many more blooms that survive, squirting jets of acid from within their bell-shaped clusters of petals. However, the black glass of Ophidian armour is unaffected by the corrosive fluid and barely a drop penetrates between the plates to sting your flesh. You emerge unscathed on the other side of the flower bed. Now there is nothing to stop you making for the Vitreous Citadel. Turn to **336**.

63

You pull the glowing sphere from your backpack and cup it in your hands. Instantly you are mesmerized by the myriad visions, so tiny and yet so detailed, that swarm within the Aleph. The longer you gaze, the more you can see: strange creatures, alien peoples, towns, continents, planets, swirling stars. You feel yourself being enveloped by the Aleph and transported within it. Roll one die. If you roll an even number, turn to 115; if you roll an odd number, turn to 126.

64

Just as the Black Shadow is about to drop on to you, your sword-blade arcs through the air and splits the creature's skull. You press yourself back against the stone wall and watch the monster's body flutter down the side of the tower like a torn rag. Restore 1 point of LUCK. Treading carefully on the worn steps, you continue upwards. Turn to 318.

65

Semeion stares in amazement at the teeming visions in the glowing sphere. 'It *is* the Aleph!' he whispers after a long silence. 'I have never known whether it was real or merely a legend. But this is undeniably it. It is beyond my powers to explain. It is, quite simply, everything – the entire Macrocosmos in this small ball. I have heard that its bearer can move into it and thus travel between worlds – but of course you know this. You carry a great burden, my friend.' You explain how you came by the Aleph: that the previous bearer entrusted it to you; that with his dying breath he mentioned the name of Globus, whom you take to be the Aleph's owner; that the Spectral Stalkers are pursuing you. If you have collected some objects during your travels, you can ask Semeion if any of them have any special meaning – turn to 235. Alternatively, you can ask instead for information about Globus – turn to 308.

66

The villagers are overjoyed that a brave warrior is prepared to help them, but they call tell you no more than the way to Mayrek's cave. You set off and after a long trudge across the dunes you find yourself climbing a wooded hillside. When you come to an avenue of clay statues you know you are nearing your goal. You walk up the winding path, marvelling at the skill of the artist who has modelled these fantastical creatures of clay. You turn the last corner and find that the avenue ends at a cave in the face of a cliff. The mouth of the cave has been blocked with boulders and rubble. The largest of the clay statues, shaped in the likeness of a misshapen, slab-faced giant, stands astride the cave-mouth. As you approach, the statue growls like thunder and begins to move! A voice from within the cave can be heard shouting: 'Stay clear! I am Mayrek, and I know what my Clay Golem can do. Run for your life!' With slow, lumbering strides, the Golem steps towards a waterfall that cascades down the cliff-face. For a few seconds it stands under the pouring water – and then, slick and glistening, it is rushing towards you. If you have a vial of Siccator, and wish to use it, turn to **204**. If you stand and fight, turn to **131**. If you choose to run away, turn to **13**.

67

The doorway does not say another word; the bridge stops swaying. You step forward gingerly. The stone slab is as firm and stable as when you first stepped on to it. You conclude that you gave the correct answer, and a glance upwards at the ornate carvings over the doorway confirms this conclusion. You hurry across the bridge and through the doorway. You have succeeded in entering the Vitreous Citadel. Turn to **189**.

68

As you advance, the Feliti back away, baring their fangs and yelping. Individually the creatures are no match for you, but it will be difficult to drive off the entire pack of them. In the fading light the swaying of the tall grass shows that they are circling you – and then the three largest of them come for you.

	SKILL	STAMINA
First FELITI	5	3
Second FELITI	4	5
Third FELITI	6	5

Fight them one at a time. Before each Attack Round, roll one die. If you roll a 1 or 2, the first Feliti attacks you; on a 3 or 4, the second; a 5 or 6, the third. If you kill one of them, turn to **109**; if not, at the end of four Attack Rounds turn to **169**.

69

You break free of the sticky filaments before the Spider can reach you. The monstrous creature retreats into its web as you make for a corner of the courtyard out of range of the Spider's trailing strands. Now you have time to consider your next move: there are four exits from the courtyard – a doorway in the middle of each wall. You are sure that if you move quickly you can reach one before the Spider can trap you. Only one of the doorways has the circle and triangle symbol above it; you face towards that doorway and make your decision. You can go through the doorway you are facing (turn to **317**); the doorway behind you (turn to **15**); the doorway to your right (turn to **285**); or the doorway to your left (turn to **367**).

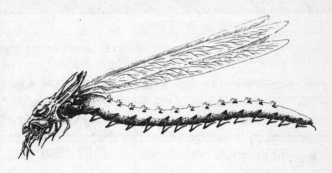

70

You feel as visible as a fly on a whitewashed wall as you climb up the blank face of the tower. The stairway seems to spiral upwards for ever, and its weatherbeaten steps of crumbling stone make you all too aware of the drop below you. In the distance you see, swooping in and out of other towers, the inhabitants of this part of the Ziggurat World. They are known as Black Shadows, because they fly silently, their wiry bodies supported by a membrane of black skin that connects their long tails, legs, arms and ears. You are just thinking how lucky you are none of them are close enough to see you when you hear a rushing of air and a flapping of membranous skin – a Black Shadow is descending on you. The creature lands above you, then, clinging to the stones with its talons, it scuttles down towards you, fangs bared. Unlike the Black Shadow, you have no way to secure yourself on to the stonework and if you fight the creature you will certainly be dislodged from the stairway. You will have to deliver a single well-aimed blow. If you have a silver dagger, it might be particularly effective against this monster – turn to **28**; if not, you must use your sword – turn to **106**.

71

You uncork the little bottle and pass it to Grondel, telling him to drink half of the liquid. You consume the remainder. You cannot detect any change in your body; all you can do is wait, and hope that the Siccator will be able to protect you from the effects of the poison. On the dais above you the Elven priest's incantations reach a loud climax. There are a few seconds of silence, then you hear the gurgling rumble of water rushing through old pipes, and a sheet of liquid splashes all round you. You grit your teeth in the expectation of pain – but you don't even feel wet. The water runs off your skin as if you had a second, invisible skin, and when the flow from the spout ceases you and Grondel are both completely dry and completely undamaged. Turn to **245**.

72

'Wrong!' barks the Logic Dog. 'I'm going to attack! You guessed incorrectly, and therefore I *will* attack.' With that, the huge beast launches itself towards you. Turn to **163**.

73

As the small voice in the back of your mind becomes more and more insistent, the beautiful visions disintegrate and fade. You blink, become fully alert and realize that you are lying on Necromon's bloodstained table. The white-coated figure has his back to you, sharpening a long knife on a grindstone. You use this opportunity to rise quietly, pick up your backpack and tiptoe away. The nearest door is the one through which Necromon entered the room earlier. You slip through it; turn to **366**.

74

The Ranganathans are between you and the door. You charge towards them and knock them aside, but their razor-sharp fingers lacerate you as you flee. Lose 4 STAMINA points. You jump over heaps of books and through the doorway, slamming the door shut behind you. As you retrace your steps along the corridor the Ranganathans open the door of their room and poke their heads out, giggling and squealing at your ignominious retreat. You arrive back at the crossroads and begin the long hike along another corridor; turn to either **164**, **243** or **373**.

75

You have very little time in which to judge which way you should jump and, having decided, you will have to jump well and with alacrity in order to avoid the crazed Colepod's charge. Roll two dice and add 2 to the result: if the total is less than your SKILL, turn to **349**; if the total is equal to, or more than, your SKILL, turn to **242**.

76

You stand in the path of the massive and grotesque war-beasts and wave your arms. The gigantic riders seem to stare straight through you and remain oblivious to you even as their steeds bear down on you. Although the beasts' hoofbeats are still unnervingly noiseless, you can see from their imprints in the turf that their hooves are as heavy and powerful as they look. You are about to be trampled; you cannot stay where you are, so you decide to attempt to grab the harness of one of the animals and pull yourself to safety. Roll two dice. If the total is less than your SKILL score, turn to **161**; if the total is equal to or more than your SKILL score, turn to **387**.

77

As you step towards the multicoloured clusters of glass flowers you are entranced by their sparkling brightness and by the musical tinkling they make as they sway in the breeze – and then you realize that there is not a breath of wind. It is your presence that is exciting the flowers, and they become a storm-tossed sea of poly-chrome scintillation as you stand before the bell-shaped blooms. Suddenly a jet of fluid shoots from the mouth of one of the flowers. You throw yourself backwards just in time as the whole bank of blooms releases a battery of liquid spray. You dip a corner of cloth into a puddle of the stuff, and the material shrivels and smokes. As you suspected, the flowers are deadly: they spray corrosive acid. However, unless you want to return to the path to face a Silica Serpent (turn to **162**), you have no choice but to try to force a passage through the flowers, cutting a swathe with your sword as you go (turn to **390**). This might prove less dangerous if you have an Umbrella (turn to **208**), or if you are wearing a suit of Ophidian armour (turn to **62**).

78

You walk for only a short time before you reach another portal. Through it you find a small rectangular chamber, on the floor of which are the remains of a camp fire. The ashes are cold, but the very thought that someone could be lost in this maze long enough to make camp for at least one night is enough to worry you. You decide to press on with all speed. There are four doorways, one in each of the walls, and as usual one of them is marked with the symbol of a triangle surmounted by a circle. You face towards it and choose which of the doorways you will leave through:

The door facing you	Turn to **285**
The door behind you	Turn to **122**
The door to your right	Turn to **257**
The door to your left	Turn to **247**

79

Fate decrees that you are going to drink water. You are a little disgruntled, but Fate has been kind to you (the ale is drugged!). You finish your meal, wash it down with the water and relax on the mattress. Lulled by the lapping of the river water below your room, you drift into sleep. Turn to **195**.

80

You put the Horn to your lips and blow. If this is the first time you have tried to deter Black Shadows by sounding the Hunting-Horn, turn to **46**; if you have tried this before, turn to **381**.

81

'You are the last pawn to be placed on the field,' you hear Drawenna say, 'and now the rules of battle change. The winning side — white or black — is the one with more surviving warriors when no more can be killed in battle. Each side plays in turn, and in one turn only a single pawn may move, but all pawns from that side may attack. A pawn may move one square ahead or either side; you may not move backwards, or diagonally, or into a square occupied by another living warrior of either side. During one side's turn, the other side's pawns cannot attack; they can only defend themselves by turning their backs on their attackers — an effective defence because of the armour. Attacking pawns can attack all enemy pawns on all adjacent squares, including those diagonally adjacent. Therefore, as you can see, a pawn attacked from one side is invulnerable, but a pawn attacked from two opposite sides is doomed to

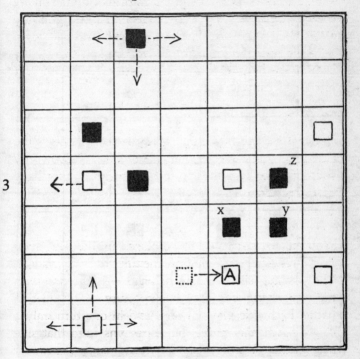

EXAMPLES OF PLAY

1. Black pawn, showing legal moves.
2. White pawn, showing legal moves.
3. In this position, the white pawn has only one legal move, as shown.
4. It is white's turn. He moves his pawn A as shown, and can now attack. Black pawns X and Y are killed, because they are directly between white pawns. Black pawn Z is safe.

The situation immediately after Drawenna (white) has placed her last pawn on the board. *You* — marked with an X, on square *F4* — are Drawenna's last pawn.

Now it is white's turn to move one pawn, and then attack. Can white win?

die. Now: to battle, my white pawns! We can yet win this game!'

The positions of the pawns are shown on the diagram opposite. You are the white pawn, marked with a cross, on the square numbered *F4* on the diagram. Your white comrades appeal to you for guidance. 'Only one of us can move in each turn,' says the warrior on square *G6*, 'and it will have to be me. I am almost surrounded; my only possible move is to my left [to G5]. If I don't move, the black warrior next to you will move along-side me, and I'll be slaughtered!'

'No!' says the warrior on square *E6*. 'I should be the one to move. If I move forward [to D6], we'll have one of these black swine diagonally between us. Or,' he con-tinues, more thoughtfully, 'if you move to your left [to F3], to keep out of danger, we can still finish off the one black warrior between me and the other fellow.'

They are waiting for your decision. If you decide that the white warrior on square *G6* should move to *G5*, turn to **398**. If you agree that the warrior on *E6* should move forward to *D6*, turn to **303**. If you think that you should be the one to move, turn to **326**. (Make a note of this reference number (**81**); it may be helpful to refer to the diagram again.)

82

You batter the glowing surface of the Prism, but your blows are futile. Your weapon rebounds from the crystal of light as if you were striking solid steel. As the Spectral Stalkers lurch in your direction, you become frantic with fear, clawing at the transparent Prism with your bare hands, but only inanimate objects, moving slowly, can penetrate the force field. As the tentacles of a Spectral Stalker seize your legs, your last sight is of the Archmage's gloating face. You have failed, and Globus has gained the Aleph.

You emerge on to a steep and rocky path that meanders down a mountainside. At the foot of the mountain you come upon a small town. It is market day, and the narrow main street is crowded with townsfolk and farmers. The stalls are selling farm produce – vegetables, honey, oil and chickens – and you can see nothing that seems significant to you. The last stall in the street, however, has a display of earthenware and metal goods. In pride of place is a finely-crafted, circular bronze plate, which somehow reminds you of the Aleph. The scene engraved across it is a depiction of the Hunt of the Gods that is an exact portrayal of the giants and the war-beasts that you encountered. The stallholder wants 3 Gold Pieces for the plate and is not prepared to haggle. If you have enough money, and want to buy the plate, record the transaction on your *Adventure Sheet*. You have now reached the end of the town; there is nothing to do but wander into the countryside and use the Aleph to travel elsewhere. Turn to **30**.

84

Even the pain in your bursting lungs cannot prevent you from slipping away. Bubbles of air foam your mouth; almost unconscious, you breathe in again – and fill your chest with cold sea water. Your adventure ends here.

85

You offer no resistance as one of the soldiers lurches behind you and brings the haft of his battle-axe down on your head. For a moment the grinning face of the gigantic warlord Syzuk seems to spin about you. As you drop into unconsciousness you are dimly aware of bony hands grasping you and carrying you away. Turn to **215**.

86

You can climb no further. Your limbs are shaking, your fingers and toes are lacerated and numb and your muscles are screaming at you to rest. You look up: the cave-mouth is still many metres above you. You look down: there is a dizzying drop to the foot of the wall of rock. You cannot move, but you cannot hope to cling to the bare stone much longer. Your only hope is to call for help. You fill your lungs and start to shout. *Test your Luck*. If you are Lucky, turn to **299**; if you are Unlucky, turn to **399**.

87

The continuous glow of light banishes your fears and makes the toys look completely ordinary. You relax on the bed; if you have Provisions, you can eat one meal if you wish, and restore up to 4 points of STAMINA. In the morning, you wake to find sunlight streaming into the room. As you prepare to leave, you glance at the little clown in his glass sphere. You can take him with you if you want to – he reminds you of the Aleph, which you decide to use immediately to take you away from this haunted castle. Turn to **61**.

88

'If you are a friend of the tyrant Globus,' shrills the Mantir, while his comrades shake their spears angrily, 'you are no friend of the people of the plains. We pay our tribute, which grows more onerous each year. We will offer no more to Globus, or give aid to his spies and other agents such as you. I intend to find out what you are, and why you are trespassing here on our lands; but we must return now to our herd. You will come with us; I will interrogate you later.' Four of the Mantirs close round you – but at that moment one of the others shrieks in alarm, and points skywards. Turn to **388**.

89

The Spectral Stalker has failed to find you. You heave a sigh of relief as the hideous creature shakes its great head in frustration and begins to dissolve into the air once more. Shivering with fear, you lie awake until the grey light of dawn appears in the cracks between the shutters. Turn to 40.

90

At last the door is free of fungus and the latch is uncovered – but you cannot see it. Drowning in a sea of black, viscous smog, your eyes blinded by tears of pain and your lungs filled with poisonous fumes, you scrabble weakly at the wooden door – but you fail to find the latch before you are overcome. Your adventure ends here.

91

Taking the Aleph from your backpack you cup it in your hands and gaze into it. The infinite display of distant worlds and alien landscapes has lost none of its power to fascinate you. The shifting visions extend into the distance in all directions – you are surrounded by the Aleph, and you feel yourself being transported within it. Roll one die. If you roll an even number, turn to 145; if you roll an odd number, turn to 156.

92

Avoiding occasional Wood Elf settlements you walk downhill, through the forest, for many hours. You find a few wild berries to eat, but they merely prevent your STAMINA being reduced by your exertions. At last the trees thin out, and you emerge from the woodlands and start across a bleak moor. The soil becomes increasingly sandy and, eventually, you see the sea. On your right, the sheer cliffs are, if anything, closer now. You see no living thing, but soon you come upon a ruined town and the footprints of several large creatures. Out at sea a cluster of huge bubbles rests on the water's surface. The beach peters out between the sea and the cliff. You see that there is a path which zig-zags up the face of the cliff. Will you take the path (turn to 12), or walk down to the shore to look at the vast bubbles (turn to 230)?

'Globus?' barks the Dragon. 'Spectral Stalkers? Never heard of them. But that's not surprising, you know. There are more books in the Library in Limbo than there are grains of sand on all the beaches in the Macrocosmos. We have at least one copy of every book ever written, and even I can't be expected to read them all. What sort of thing is a Globus? Or a Spectral Stalker?' You confess that you don't know what a Spectral Stalker is, but that Globus is an Archmage. 'An Archmage? If he's of any note at all he'll warrant an entry in the *Directory of Wizards*. You'll find a copy a couple of kilometres along that corridor there. You can't miss it, it's a big black book with the word *Wizards* on the spine. Well, run along then.' Will you follow the Dragon's pointing finger (turn to 373), or would you rather set off in another direction to explore the corridors of the Library (turn to 275)?

94

You throw yourself to the ground and the jet of fluid only just misses you. As you roll away from the Silica Serpent you hear a strange hissing noise, and you look up to see that the rocks that have been sprayed by the Silica Serpent's venom are bubbling, steaming and dissolving into smoke. You pick yourself up, step back — and immediately collide with the leader of a troop of soldiers. They are tall, thin humanoids, totally encased in plate armour made entirely of black glass. Each carries a spear and has a set of pipes hanging from his belt. You are trapped between the soldiers and the Silica Serpent; you have no choice but to surrender. Turn to 306.

95

Suddenly there is no floor beneath your feet. The whole base of the tunnel has dropped into a pit — and you are falling after it! The vast stone slab lands with a grinding crash and a second later, with a relatively unimpressive thud, you land on top of it. Roll one die and deduct the result from your STAMINA. If you

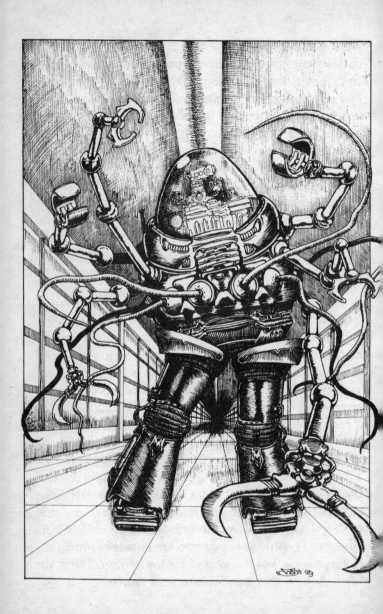

are still alive, you can see that you and the stone floor have fallen several metres, and you cannot see any way of climbing up. Then you feel the floor move again, and you realize that the entire slab is rising, lifting you upwards. After several minutes of slow, juddering ascent the floor returns to its original position and you are once again facing the strange design carved into the wall at the tunnel's end. This time, will you press the right 'eye' (turn to 290), or the left one (turn to 216)? Or will you decide instead to retrace your steps along the tunnel (turn to 122)?

turn to 290), or the left one (turn to 216)? Or will you decide instead to retrace your steps along the tunnel (turn to 122)?

96

A whining noise fills the air, and one of the room's metallic walls slides upwards to reveal a vast vaulted hall, ribbed with girders of shining steel and lined with metal cages. Trudging towards you between the lines of cages is a nightmarish monster. It is twice as tall as you, with legs that look like part of a giant's suit of armour, and instead of feet it has, at the end of each leg, a row of wheels that turn a band of metal plates. Its head is a transparent dome within which lights flash and wheels turn and, worst of all, from its torso sprouts a mass of long steel limbs, some flexible and no thicker than a ship's hawser, others jointed and terminating in pincers. 'Grappler reporting from Transporter Bay,' the monster says in a monotone. 'Intruder located.' It advances towards you; you have no choice but to fight. If you have a weapon named Extinguisher, and wish to use it, turn to 280; otherwise turn to 389.

97

You stand, breathless, over the innkeeper's body. If you need a new weapon you may take his sword. You look towards the last red glimmer of the sunset – and freeze in horror. The hideous shape of a Spectral Stalker is forming in the air, towering above you on four fleshless legs. The glittering orbs of its eyes search back and forth and below them the writhing mass of tentacles seems to be sensing your scent on the air. Add one point to your TRAIL score, and then *Test your Trail score*. Roll three dice. If the total is equal to or more than your TRAIL score, turn to 5; if the total is less than your TRAIL score, turn to 307.

98

Holding your breath at every step, you climb upwards. You reach the sixteenth step without feeling the slightest tremor. With great care, you leap over the seventeenth without touching it and land on the eighteenth step. Nothing happens and you advance confidently – but only as far as the twentieth step, where an electrical charge as powerful as a bolt of lightning fries you in an instant. The adventure ends here for warriors who fail to calculate correctly.

99

Semeion pulls the helmet from his head, and indicates that you should do likewise. Then he crosses the chamber and takes from a shelf two large glass jars. Each jar contains what looks like a gigantic red slug. 'These are Energy Leeches,' Semeion says, plunging his hand into one of the jars and extracting its writhing occupant.

'They suck vital resources from the body,' he adds, coiling fine wire around one Leech and then the other, 'but the salts can be restored by drinking sea water.' When both are cocooned in wire, he places the mouth of one of them against his bared arm and grimaces in distaste as its teeth sink into his flesh. He fastens the other Leech to your arm in the same way. Then, together, you and he place the helmets over your heads. Immediately you feel the strength draining from your body. Roll one die; make a note of the result, and deduct it from your STAMINA. These lost points can be restored only by a drink of sea water. If you now have no remaining STAMINA points turn to 203; otherwise, turn to 250.

100

'A wise choice,' Mayrek says, handing you the little box. 'Gold is always of use. This particular item has a little of my skill worked into it: the pattern of the decoration on the box has powers to assist you in difficulties.' Add 1 point to your current LUCK score, and 1 point to your *Initial* LUCK as well; and don't forget to add 5 Gold Pieces to your *Adventure Sheet*. You thank Mayrek and depart along the avenue of statues. When you are out of sight of the cave, you wonder where to go next. There seems to be no choice but to use the Aleph to leave this place. Turn to 211.

101

After walking only a short distance you step through a doorway, beyond which you find two more open doorways, with a tunnel beyond each. By the half-light that creeps in through a fissure high above, you can see that one of the three doorways has the circle and triangle symbol inscribed above it. Facing this doorway, you have to choose whether to go through the portal in front of you (turn to **367**); the one behind you (turn to **317**); or the one to your right (turn to **26**).

You are exhausted. Your limbs are trembling, every muscle in your body aches and your fingers and toes are numb. Worse, you are scarcely more than half-way to the top of the cliff. Dizzy and weak, you pull yourself on to a ledge that is just wide enough for you to stand on; and there you remain, clinging to the cliff and incapable of movement, your face pressed against the cold stone. After what seems like hours you hear a noise: a flapping, as of the wings of giant birds. You turn your head and find yourself staring into the malevolent red eyes of a Black Shadow, one of the bloodsucking, membrane-winged creatures that inhabit part of the second level of this world. You have no strength to resist as it plucks you from the ledge and carries you into the sky. You lose consciousness – and wake as you are being flung to the floor of a gloomy circular crypt. As you pick yourself up you hear the sound of the door being locked and barred. You are a prisoner; but, as you idly kick the straw that is scattered across the floor, you find a trapdoor set into the flagstones. This seems to be your only escape route – turn to **140**.

103

'You're from Khul?' says Wayland. 'Khul, on the world of Titan? I know of it, of course. Primitive technology, compared to some worlds I could name, but an interesting place all the same. You are wet, aren't you? Sorry about that – I just can't resist a joke. Have a swig of this; it'll dry you out in no time.' Wayland's hand dwarfs the bottle that he offers you. If you accept this offer, turn to **356**. If you decline to drink from the bottle, Wayland is not offended – turn to **175**.

104

The largest of the Vaskind advances on you, his sword whistling through the air as he thrashes it from side to side. 'Single combat,' he grunts. 'If you live, you go free.'

VASKIND   SKILL 7   STAMINA 9

If you are still alive after two rounds of combat, add 1 point to your TRAIL score. The five Vaskind who have been watching your fight in solemn silence suddenly cry out and run into the sea. Their leader backs away from you with a look of horror on his frog-like face. The hideous shape of a Spectral Stalker is forming in the air, towering above you on four fleshless legs. As it materializes the glittering orbs of its eyes search back and forth, and its tentacles seem to be sensing your scent on the air. *Test your Trail score.* Roll three dice. If the total is equal to or more than your TRAIL score, turn to **60**; if the total is less than your TRAIL score, turn to **300**.

105

Gasps of astonishment; then laughter, cheers and finally applause! You have appeared on stage, in front of an audience, inside an open-fronted cabinet like a sentry-box. You step forward and are greeted with another burst of applause. The stage is in fact a roofed wagon, open along one side. Standing next to you is the Conjuror, a tall, saturnine figure in a black cloak, and his assistant, a young woman dressed as a cat. Before you is the audience, a crowd of peasants still open-mouthed in amazement at your appearance. At the back of the throng stands an open carriage containing a plump nobleman who is staring, not at you, but at the empty seat beside him. Even the Conjuror seems surprised to see you, but he recovers and addresses his audience: 'Ladies and gentlemen! A double miracle! Not only have I spirited the Baron's beautiful daughter from her seat in his coach; I have also caused this warrior to appear in the magic cabinet! Have no fear, my Lord, your daughter will be restored to you in just a few moments. Meanwhile my assistant will escort this warrior backstage — Felice, take our visitor away!' His assistant, as graceful as the animal she resembles, draws aside the curtain at the rear of the stage and beckons to you — and in that moment you glimpse her long furry tail, and realize that it is not part of her costume! Felice is not a woman — perhaps she is a Were-cat. Will you accompany her backstage (turn to 310), or will you jump from the stage and try to escape into the crowd (turn to 177)?

106

Bracing yourself as securely as you can on the precarious steps, you make ready to strike as soon as the Black Shadow is within range. Roll four dice. If the result is less than the sum of your SKILL and LUCK, turn to **64**; if the result is equal to, or greater than, the sum of your SKILL and LUCK, turn to **394**.

107

Anticipating an easy victory over the frail-looking Mapmaker, you charge across the study towards him – only to be met by crackling lines of sparks that shoot from his metal fingers. 'The power of Science can easily be turned into a force for destruction!' Metron announces grimly as he wheels his thin frame towards you. Howling in pain each time one of the sparks strikes your body, you back towards the glowing chamber from which you emerged. Roll one die and subtract the result from your STAMINA. Also add 1 point to your TRAIL score. The chamber is behind you; you step backwards into it and hope that it will transport you elsewhere. Turn to **42**.

108

'All I ask,' says Necromon, 'is a little of your life-force. Don't be alarmed! A strong warrior like you has energy to spare; you won't even notice the difference. Nor is the extraction of the life-force painful or in any way unpleasant. On the contrary! The potion that I will use to free your spirit, so that I can trap a little of it in my glass, has the power to bring enlightenment. Visions, dreams, bliss – all these will be yours, my friend.

Simply drink this potion and then keep the flask firmly to your lips, so that I may hold there a little portion of your essential spirit.' If you are willing to agree to this procedure, turn to **249**; if you insist that you must leave, turn to **9**.

109

There is a moment of silence as the lean body of the dead Feliti slumps to the ground. The whistle of the wind in the tall grass sounds like the keening of a multitude of lost souls. Then, with a chorus of enraged baying, the entire pack of Feliti hurl themselves at you. You cannot kill them all; your adventure ends here.

110

In this round of combat you decide to let fate take its course. *Test your Luck*. If you are Unlucky, your sword slides uselessly along the Silica Serpent's scaly flank — return to **287** and continue your fight with the creature. If you are Lucky, turn to **238**.

111

The old woman tosses the coins into the air and they disappear. You hear a distant metallic tinkle, as if the coins had reappeared and landed in a nearby cavern. 'Listen to the words of the Oracle!' the crone intones. 'You, warrior, have been within a dream. And no ordinary mortal's dream, but the dream of a god. Which god? That I know not, for there are many gods in the Macrocosmos. But I hazard that he is a god of hunting! While inside his dream you acquired his Horn — not the most potent of items to steal from a god, but perhaps it will be useful. Sound it when you are faced with danger; it will deter those opponents who fear loud noises, at least. And now you must depart, for your pursuers are ever vigilant. Before you leave, accept this charm.' The old woman traces a pattern in the air; regain 1 point of LUCK. 'I know,' she continues, 'that you have your own means of travelling, so I will refrain from advising you; but if, as I suspect, you are collecting signs and portents that have to do with your burden, I suggest that the market in the town below my cave might be of interest.' The fires flare up, then die – and the old woman has gone. The exit from the cave is revealed by a distant glimmer of daylight; you can leave through it (turn to **83**), or use the Aleph to travel elsewhere (turn to **30**).

112

You pull the Aleph from your backpack and cup it in your hands, but all you see within it are dull grey clouds. The Black Shadows are all about you, but they seem to recognize the Aleph, for they retreat. You are still hemmed in, however, and, after chattering amongst themselves for a few seconds, the Black Shadows advance on you again. This time they are careful not to damage you too severely with their talons, as if determined to take you alive; restore 1 point of LUCK. In the end, however, although you slaughter many of them in your heroic stand at the base of the tower, their inexhaustible supply of reinforcements ensures that there can be only one outcome. You are overwhelmed, swamped beneath black folds of skin and you feel sharp fangs pierce your flesh. The venom works quickly and you drift into unconsciousness. Turn to 291.

113

Sitting at the table, you grab a hunk of bread and a slice of meat and stuff them into your mouth. The food is very tasty (you may restore up to 4 points of STAMINA). Now you need something to drink. The ale is very tempting, but you know that to keep a clear head you should drink only a little water. You spy a small copper coin on the floor and decide to let fate choose your beverage. On one side of the coin is the head of a queen. *Heads I drink the ale*, you say to yourself, and toss the coin into the air. *Test your Luck*. If you are Lucky, the coin lands head down; turn to 79. If you are Unlucky, the coin lands head up; turn to 312.

114

The Spectral Stalker's tentacles writhe in frustration as it dissolves into the air. As you recover from the shock of seeing the ghostly demon, so do the Ophidians and you are once again surrounded. Now, however, the black-armoured beings seem to treat you with wary respect, and are no longer inclined to take revenge for your assault on their comrade. Four of them stand guard on you while the rest return to the trapped Silica Serpent. Turn to 133.

115

By the light of a hundred flickering torches you see that you are in a city of crumbling stone buildings. The courtyard is full of the city's Elven inhabitants. You look up to the dark sky, but you can see only the distant crags and folds of a rocky vault. The entire city is enclosed within a huge cavern and the Elves are all staring at you with saucer-shaped eyes that are adapted to life underground. You are standing at the foot of the dais on which sits the huge, moss-encrusted stone head of a grotesque idol; an Elven priest stands beside it. The mouth of the deity is carved into the shape of a spout; below it, next to you, there is a shallow pool. Standing in the pool, chained by the ankles so he cannot move from beneath the spout, is an aged Elf.

The priest stares at you, and then begins to laugh. 'So, Grondel,' he sneers down at the chained Elf, 'this is your so-called proof of your heretical doctrine of other worlds. This looks like a pitiful creature to me and is no evidence of other realms beyond our Cave. But no doubt if it is a powerful being, it will protect you from the wrath of Vacavon. Guards! Seize this creature! Chain him with Grondel beneath the mouth of Vacavon!' Guards with spears advance towards you. If you have a rune-inscribed wheel-hub, and you want to produce it, turn to **331**. Otherwise, you will have to fight (turn to **3**) or surrender (turn to **301**).

116

Keeping close to the base of the enormous cliff, you walk for hours through gradually thinning woodland.

You manage to find a few edible roots to stave off your hunger, but they are insufficient to restore any STAMINA. At last you leave the trees, and finally you can see a way up the cliff: a path starts nearby and zig-zags up the face. With the cliff behind you, you look out across a vast plain of grass, its flat expanse broken only by a few gently rolling hills and an occasional low tree. Some distance away, herds of grazing animals are being shepherded by strange creatures.

There is a disturbance in the nearest herd: an animal panics, breaks away, and begins to run straight towards you. Will you advance on to the grassland to intercept the stray animal (turn to **276**); or will you turn and take the cliff-face path (turn to **12**)?

117

You trudge for hours across the dunes. There is less and less vegetation, and eventually you are walking through an arid desert. There is no shelter, and the sun is unbearably hot. You sit down to rest in a hollow between dunes — and the sand beneath you begins to move. You have disturbed a Sandsnake: a gigantic serpent that basks under a light covering of sand. As you struggle to stand, its body coils around your legs and its head rears up in front of you. You must fight it. It has two attacks in each Attack Round: the first attack is the twining of its scaly body, and unless you wound it, it will coil itself about you, reducing your SKILL by 2 points. Its second attack is with its venomous fangs, and if it wounds you you must deduct 4 points of STAMINA.

SANDSNAKE   SKILL 6   STAMINA 10

If you defeat it, you find that any Glowcandles you may have purchased have been broken in the struggle (delete them from your *Adventure Sheet*). With a sigh, you climb a dune to survey the empty desert. There seems to be no choice but to use the Aleph to leave this place. Turn to **211**.

118

You walk through the doorway into utter darkness. You take a few more steps forward – only to hear the door slam shut behind you. You are trapped. Lights begin to glow feebly. Turn to **392**.

119

The Minstrel slaps the strings of his harp and the rhythmic chant issuing from the instrument's carved mouth rises in pitch. Flailing their limbs in time with the song and bellowing with fear and frustration, the Zwinian courtiers and townsfolk are forced to form a long line and dance up to the battlements. At the front of the line Frampa is trembling with the effort of trying to resist the harp's enchantment; but he cannot prevent himself leading his people on to the narrow ledge that overlooks an almost vertical drop at the edge of the plateau. The Minstrel strikes his hand across the strings of the harp, creating a loud jangling discord. With cries of despair Frampa and his people find themselves leaping from the battlements and into the void. Smiling, the Minstrel listens to the fading cries. Then there is silence, and you are alone with the Minstrel. 'My thanks for your assistance, stranger,' he says, 'but I no longer need you.' As he draws his sword, he speaks the words that undo his spell and you see your opponent for the first time: Barogkaz the Enchanter, a gigantic Zwinian. His snout wrinkles in a sneer, and he attacks.

BAROGKAZ   SKILL 9   STAMINA 13

If you are still alive after five rounds of combat, turn to **193**.

A flock of Black Shadows descends on you, flapping around you like animated sheets. They seem reluctant to rend you with their talons and, whirling and slashing at them, you are able to fend them off for a while. But at last you are overwhelmed, smothered in dark folds of skin, and you feel sharp fangs plunging into your flesh. The venom in their bites starts to work at once and you drift into unconsciousness. Turn to **291**.

121

As you step into the blackness of the tunnel you realize your mistake: the rough floor slopes downwards! You stumble, slide and fall into a doorless chamber that smells of smoke and ash, losing 2 points of STAMINA. You hear a faint echo of Syzuk's triumphant shout: 'Advance no further, my warriors. The foolish creature has fallen into the fire-pit. He is in the belly of mighty Glund. Let him be sacrificed forthwith! Our victory is assured!'

You jump to reach the tunnel entrance, but it is high in the wall of the chamber and you cannot reach it. Syzuk and his Skeletal Warriors continue chanting. You become aware that the chamber is uncomfortably warm. Spirals of smoke issue from cracks in the walls and the soles of your boots are becoming unbearably hot. You are about to be baked inside a god! For a moment you panic, and then you remember the Aleph. You retrieve it from your pack: in the darkness of the chamber its minute moving landscapes shine with brilliant light. As you look into it, the Aleph expands to surround you and the breathless heat fades. Roll one die: if you roll an even number, turn to **51**. If you roll an odd number, turn to **36**.

122

Once again you find yourself walking in near-darkness along a seemingly endless tunnel. At last you see light ahead and step out of the end of the tunnel into a square courtyard. Sunlight streams down the shaft made by the four walls and sparkles on the spouting waters of the fountain at the centre of the courtyard. The fountain is a statue carved in the likeness of a muscular man with the horned head of a bull; the clear liquid shoots from his uplifted mouth, splashes down his athletic torso and collects in the stone basin in which he stands. You approach the fountain: the liquid is transparent, colourless and odourless – it seems to be pure water. If you want to drink from the basin, turn to 277; if not, turn to 20.

123

Your sword strikes one of the Silica Serpent's eyes, which shatters into a thousand shards. A fountain of black fluid jets from the creature's eye-socket as it dies. You wipe your sword and continue along the path towards the Vitreous Citadel. Turn to 336.

124

You take the Aleph from your backpack. Cupping it between your hands, you are instantly mesmerized by the countless tiny visions which swarm within its infinite depths. The longer you gaze, the more you can see: farmlands and deserts, monstrous creatures and vast gleaming machines, rainbow-ringed planets and spiralling galaxies of stars. You feel yourself being enveloped by the Aleph, and transported within it. Roll one die. If you roll an even number, turn to **180**; if you roll an odd number, turn to **105**.

You approach the net cautiously, expecting it to contain a savage animal. As you begin to cut through the ropes, however, you are astonished to find that the captive is akin to the winged humanoid which dropped out of the sky above Khul and died at your feet – the one who entrusted the Aleph to your care and started you on your travels between worlds. He has the bright robes and wide eyes of his fellow, but his wings are made of long white feathers like a swan's. One of his legs is bent at an unnatural angle beneath his prone body, and you guess that it is broken. 'My thanks for aiding me, warrior,' he whispers, 'but you must not remain here. I know who you are, and I know the burden you carry. Flocks of Silica Serpents will be here ere long and you must not be discovered, still less taken by them. Leave me, hide yourself – quickly!'

If you want to ignore his advice and carry him to the shelter of the woods, turn to **37**; if you leave him, you run from the clearing and make for the higher ground nearer the cliffs – turn to **190**.

126

Under a cloudless blue sky, the park extends to the horizon in every direction. The lush grass is dotted with spinneys of oaks and elms and there are larger patches of woodland that cover the gently rolling hills. Not a branch stirs; no bird's song disturbs the silence. As you approach the edge of the wood, the undergrowth is thrown into a turmoil of movement as a bizarre assortment of wildlife bursts from the cover of the trees. Deer, rabbits, hares, foxes, badgers, boar and even brown bears, and with them are horned goat-legged Satyrs, green-skinned Nymphs, Centaurs and a Unicorn. All are running, fleeing from the wood, scattering in panic across the park, open-mouthed with fear but as silent as shadows. They run past, barely noticing you in their headlong flight. You look again towards the wood and see their terrible pursuers. Armoured giants on horned war-beasts emerge from between the trees, galloping relentlessly but as silently as their prey. The giants, noble and cruel-featured, are clothed in ornate bejewelled costumes, their weapons sparkling in the sunlight. Their red-eyed steeds seem to skim the grass. If you want to stand in the path of these hunters and try to attract their attention, turn to **76**; if you decide to stand well clear, turn to **358**.

127

As you descend the stairs, you hear a rhythmic clanking. You stop in amazement as you see what appears to be a moving suit of armour with a square head and flashing eyes climbing the steps towards you. It stops, elevates its metal head, and speaks in a voice like iron rubbing against stone. 'You're lucky you caught me,' it drones. 'I was just going out on my rounds. Are you lost? You've come to the right place. Ha ha ha. Follow me. This way.'

The metal man turns and leads you into a cellar full of junk. At a glance you see hats, cloaks, boxes, parcels, weapons, scrolls, purses and hundreds of unrecognizable objects, all jumbled together in a heap. Black things like bats on sticks hang from hooks in the ceiling. There are caged animals, statues, chairs, a clock and a doorway on whose lintel is engraved the word *EXIT*.

'My name's Lost Property,' the metal man continues. 'Seeing as that's what I am. Where I come from I was Domestic Robot Number 45B, but there's no call for Domestic Robots here in Limbo. So I live down here and keep the Library tidy. Look at all this stuff I've collected! Do you need anything? Maybe we could do some business.' If you want to trade with the Robot, turn to **225**. If you decide to go through the *EXIT* doorway, turn to **185**.

128

The liquid is tasteless and you have gulped down several mouthfuls before you become aware of a growing sensation of well-being. Your wounds hurt less and the burden of fatigue is lifted from your shoulders. You drink more of the liquid, which is clearly some kind of concentrated food in fluid form, and you soon feel completely satiated. You may restore up to 6 points of STAMINA. Then, with renewed vigour, you stride up the stairs and through the door. Turn to **189**.

129

The outline of the tall shape becomes clearer, but as you stare aghast at its nightmarish appearance, it senses your presence and bounds towards you on impossibly long, thin legs. You see its twitching limbs and the glittering facets of its eyes, and then it is upon you. Snatching your sword from your scabbard you try to defend yourself against its claws, but you are too slow. Knife-sharp talons clutch you and throw you to the ground. Lose 4 STAMINA points.

You despair of escaping with your life, but the thing draws back, as if to enjoy the sight of you reeling with pain. You hear its voice like an icy whisper in your brain: 'We have the scent of your blood, human. We will find you again.' When you look up the monster has disappeared. Add 1 point to your TRAIL score.

Nursing your wounds you trudge towards the trees. It is as well that you cast a wary eye behind you from time to time: the monster, or another like it, is beginning to reappear. This time you decide not to wait and run for the shelter of the forest. Turn to 44.

130

Eventually you reach the top of the cliff, but crossing the terrain ahead of you looks even more difficult than climbing the cliff. The path peters out in a landscape of bare crags, shadowed ravines and jagged rocks. There is no vegetation; the only features are the cylindrical towers that are perched on the tallest of the rocky peaks. One of the towers, some distance away, is much larger than the others. Beyond the towers you see another wall of rock — another impossibly tall cliff, atop which is the third level of this strange world. If you want to investigate the towers, there is one rising from a nearby pinnacle of rock; turn to **353**. If you would rather make for the distant cliff, turn to **214**.

As the Golem pounds towards you, you dart between the thick clay legs and deliver a powerful blow to its thigh. Nothing happens; the monster is undamaged. You have no time to think: the mallet is rushing downwards again, and you have to dodge. This will not be a fight: all you can do is dodge the mallet-blows until the sun begins to dry the Golem's body and cause the monster to slow down. Roll one die and add three: this is the number of times you must dodge before the Golem slows. Each time you dodge, roll two dice; if the total is more than your SKILL score, you are struck a glancing blow that reduces your STAMINA by 2 points. If you survive, you are rewarded by the sight of the sun-dried Golem becoming motionless; but behind the Golem you see something much worse. The hideous shape of a Spectral Stalker is forming in the air, towering above you on four fleshless legs. Add 1 point to your TRAIL score, then *Test your Trail score*. Roll three dice. If the total is equal to or more than your TRAIL score, turn, to **255**; if the total is less than your TRAIL score, turn to **307**.

132

A golden radiance surrounds the seven objects on the table as Semeion seems to drift into a trance. 'The Spectral Stalkers have been summoned by the evil wizard Globus,' he intones in a voice that echoes as if drawn from a great distance. 'Globus has set them to find the Aleph.'

As Semeion's voice fades, a seven-pointed star appears in the midst of the objects on the table. Semeion blinks, shakes his head and smiles. 'You are indeed fortunate,' he says. 'You know now that Globus is your enemy and this Talisman has been granted to you — wear it always about your neck, for it will help to protect you against his sorcery.' Restore 1 point of LUCK and reduce your TRAIL score by 2 points while you possess the Talisman. You thank Semeion and ask him if he can give you any information about Globus. Turn to **308**.

133

Having muzzled the Silica Serpent and bound up its diaphanous wings, the Ophidians turn their attentions to you. Soon you are cocooned in ropes and slung from a pole which two Ophidians carry between them with ease. You see little of your journey except for the boulders that pass beneath you, but you are aware that the Ophidians are bringing the Silica Serpent with them. The Ophidians stop at the foot of a sheer wall of rock which they intend to climb. A concerted burst of music from their pipes is sufficient to make the Silica Serpent temporarily docile, and they release its wings so that it can hover alongside them as they climb upwards. As you have no wings they are obliged to carry you. As you are still bound in ropes you can do nothing to prevent yourself being dashed against outcrops of rock — lose 2 points of STAMINA. Within minutes the foot of the escarpment is far beneath you and then you are dragged over a stone lip and into the mouth of a cave. Two tunnels lead away into the darkness; you are carried along the left-hand passage and into a cavern full of tethered Silica Serpents, each one guarded by several Ophidians. Turn to **53**.

134

You succeed in snatching the Aleph from the Tyrant's grasping hands and run from the chamber and down dark spiral stairs. You hear the old creature blundering after you, muttering curses, and from the bottom of the tower you hear the echoes of doors slamming shut. The only way to escape is to use the Aleph: turn to **365**.

135

You are in a thick forest. The canopy of trees shuts out most of the daylight; the undergrowth hampers your movements. You start walking and are soon approaching a rough road that runs through the forest. You have almost reached the road when you hear footsteps. Crouching behind a bush, you see a lone figure trudging along the road – a young man with a small harp slung on his back. You assume he is a Minstrel. Before you can greet him, you hear heavy footfalls. Striding along the road from the other direction comes a gigantic, ungainly, two-legged lizard, ridden by a brutish warrior with the face of a boar. When the boar-face spies the Minstrel, he urges his mount into a charge. Instead of running away or defending himself, the Minstrel unslings his harp – which starts to play and sing by itself! The effect on the boar-face is instant: he sways in his saddle and almost falls. The Minstrel draws his sword to finish off his helpless attacker, but another boar-face approaches on another giant lizard and you can hear the heavy tread of a third. Will you remain hidden (turn to 233) or come to the Minstrel's aid (turn to 265)?

136

'Wrong!' roars the doorway. 'Utterly wrong! Why, foolish intruder, you have only to look at the beautiful and intricately-worked carvings that adorn the apex of my framework! There you will see my crowns. Regard them now: this will be the last sight your eyes will see!' Turn to 31.

137

A nervous squeal from the Baron's daughter alerts you to the silent opening of the cabin's inner door. The black-cloaked Conjuror stands on the threshold, his malevolent grin revealing a set of sharp teeth. His sibilant words confirm your fear that he is a Vampire. 'A very successful expedition,' he whispers. 'Not only have I captured the Baron's daughter – you, my dear, will come to my castle and become one of the loveliest of my undead brides – but I have snared an intruder whose blood will sustain me on my journey. Approach me, warrior. Look into my eyes!'

You are in a desperate plight. If you want to throw open the exterior door of the cabin and leap from the careering wagon, turn to **289**. If you have a silver dagger in your backpack, you may use it to attack the Vampire – turn to **231**. Otherwise, you will have to defend yourself as best you can – turn to **382**.

138

'So,' growls the robed Vaskind, 'you are a friend of the cruel dictator Globus. One of his spies, no doubt, sent to the lower levels to check that his subjects are cowed and subservient. We should kill you; but we are a race of warriors and we remember the honourable codes of our distant homeland. We will expel you from the dome; if you survive and reach the surface, take this message to your master: *We do not fear you, Globus, and when our Queen returns she will lead us to our revenge against you!* Now, guards – take this creature away!'

You are carried, struggling, to the edge of the dome.

As you are forced through the clinging membrane, you take a last gulp of warm air before you are plunged into the icy waters. If you have any Siccator, and think it might be useful now, turn to **357**; if not, turn to **19**.

You retreat towards the gaping mouth of the stone skull as the two soldiers clamber on to the dais and advance towards you. They are emaciated, almost like skeletons, with pale skin stretched tightly over their bones and eyes that gleam like their leader's. They move slowly, but wield their black battle-axes with unnatural ease. One of them is almost upon you: you must fight.

SKELETAL WARRIOR   SKILL 9   STAMINA 4

As you fight, you are too preoccupied to heed the strange disturbance in the air above you. The Spectral Stalkers are beginning to recognize the patterns of your mental energy: add 1 point to your TRAIL score. If you defeat the first Skeletal Warrior, there is no respite: the second is facing you, and more are climbing on to the stone ledge. You cannot fight them all. You must surrender (turn to **85**), or try to escape by running into the mouth of the stone skull (turn to **348**).

When you drop through the trapdoor you find yourself at the end of a tunnel. Following the tunnel round a corner, you find that it ends at a wooden door. You push it open to reveal a small, empty room whose walls glow with an eerie light. You step into the room, and the door closes behind you. Nothing else happens, though, so you decide to study the glowing walls. The walls and ceiling of the room are covered with a revolting fungus: thick folds of sickly white lumps that give off a pallid luminescence and a stench of rotting food. The door you entered through is covered with the stuff, so much so that you can hardly make it out. There is another door, equally blanketed with fungus, in the opposite wall. You will have to clear at least some of the fungus from this door. Will you peel off the disgusting stuff with your bare hands (turn to **347**), hack at it with your sword (turn to **48**); or, if you have a Heatsword, will you try to burn the fungus from the door (turn to **181**)?

141

Dodging the first boulder-breaking blow of the Golem's mallet, you sprinkle the Siccator in a wide arc (cross it from your *Adventure Sheet*). The drops of liquid sparkle in the air — and fall to the ground between the Golem's massive feet. You missed, and the Golem, still slick with water, attacks you again. One blow from his hand sends you sprawling in the dust — lose 2 STAMINA points. You stagger to your feet. You have only two options: run (turn to **13**) or fight (turn to **131**).

142

The iridescent monster is a Silica Serpent. It raises its head and utters a piercing screech, whereupon the Wood Elves approach and kneel in a row before it. In turn, each Elf reaches forward hesitantly and plucks one of the Serpent's glittering scales from the top of its head; then all four run off, capering and joking as they display the hard-won scales like trophies in their hats. More Silica Serpents wheel down from the skies to inspect the netted captive, then two of them lift the net into the air and the others escort them aloft. You watch until the flock of Serpents is no more than a speck in the sky, then head towards the towering cliffs. Turn to **190**.

143

The Talisman, hanging on its chain around your neck, begins to pulse with a light that is almost as bright as the dazzling beam which is crushing you. The pain seems to recede a little, as if the Talisman were absorbing some of the beam's strength. Although you can feel yourself beginning to slip away into unconsciousness, you cling to the hope that the Talisman will enable you to survive the inexorable pressure. Roll three dice. If the total is less than your STAMINA, turn to **212**; if the total is equal to, or greater than, your STAMINA, turn to **372**.

144

You pull the furled Umbrella from your backpack. Grondel asks you what it is, but you merely smile and tell him to shuffle as close to you as his shackles will allow. The large-eyed Elves in the courtyard stare in wonder at the strange device. On the dais above you, the Elven priest's incantations reach a loud climax. There are a few seconds of silence before you hear the gurgling rumble of water rushing through old pipes. With one swift movement you put up the Umbrella and

hold it aloft. As the sheet of liquid splashes all round you, you manage to remain dry, though a few drops splash on to your legs, and a little of the water seeps through your boots. The merest touch of the liquid turns skin and flesh rotten, and there is no cure. Roll one die, and deduct the result from your current *and* your *Initial* STAMINA. If you are still alive, you wait until the last drops of water have dripped from the spout, then you take down the Umbrella and grin victoriously to the amazed crowd. Turn to **245**.

145

You find yourself in a small chamber made entirely of glowing, interconnected rods. Through them you can see that the chamber is inside a complicated mechanism of whirring cogs and humming bulbs of light. One side of the chamber is open, and beyond the opening you can see a room crammed with other mechanical devices. The walls are covered with bookshelves and complex charts. A bizarre figure trundles into view — a humanoid, you decide, but only just. Riding on a self-propelled cart with four wheels, the robed being is extremely thin, so that his torso looks too small and weak to support his huge bald head. Long metal fingers protrude from the sleeves of the robe, wire meshes bulge from the sides of his head where you would expect ears to be and round glass lenses sit in his eye-sockets. 'A visitor!' he cries in a piping voice. 'It is such a long time since I last had a visitor. Quickly, step from the machine while you may!' Will you emerge from the chamber (turn to **253**), or stay inside it (turn to **42**)?

146

The path winds for hours along the face of the cliff before it finally takes you upward again. At last you reach the top of the cliff, and look across a barren landscape of rocks and gullies that rise in a series of escarpments and culminate, in the distance, in another dizzying cliff. As you set off towards this distant goal, you notice a few Silica Serpents wriggling across the turquoise sky and as you walk further into the heart of this desolate land more appear. You begin to fear that this part of the Ziggurat World is their home and that they are bound to detect your presence. Sure enough, one of the scaly creatures undulates from above and lands on the path in a gully ahead of you. You hesitate, uncertain of what to do next and realize that the Silica Serpent is in difficulties. Its wings have been snagged by something and it cannot take off again. Will you approach it (turn to **184**), or conceal yourself and wait to see what happens next (turn to **229**)?

147

The door swings open and you step across the threshold into the room. Without warning, a bucket of water falls from the top of the door: you are drenched and the bucket strikes your head as it falls. Lose 1 STAMINA point. You shake the water out of your eyes and see that you are in a small room full of half-dismantled machines. A big man, so tall that he almost has to stoop in this low-ceilinged room, is leaning against a high-backed chair and laughing so much that his eyes are as full of water as yours.

'Oh dear, oh dear,' he guffaws. 'I didn't think anybody fell for that old bucket above the door trick these days. That's cheered me up no end! You look like a drowned rat! I'm Wayland, in case you're wondering, and you're obviously a visitor. Where do you hail from?' Will you attack this sniggering practical joker (turn to **59**), or will you restrain your anger and reply to his question (turn to **103**)?

148
The tunnel is almost completely dark but you can see a glimmer of light in the distance. You head towards it and finally arrive at a small chamber with two closed doors. Round one of the doors there is a crack of light – the glimmer that you saw from afar – suggesting that the room beyond is occupied; beyond the other door there seems to be only darkness. Will you choose to try the door with light beyond it (turn to **324**), or the door to darkness (turn to **202**)?

149
The sheer cliff towers above you. The rays of the morning sun penetrate only a little distance into the tunnel beyond the portal, but once you have plunged into the gloom you are relieved to find that the darkness is alleviated at intervals by thin beams of grey light that emanate from chimneys and fissures in the roof of the tunnel. You turn to take a last look at the distant mountains and, shielding your eyes against the sunlight, you make out a symbol – a triangle surmounted by a circle – carved into the lintel above the inside of the portal. You turn again and press on into the near-darkness. Turn to **15**.

150

The Wood Elves jabber amongst themselves as you try to explain your unexpected appearance. It seems that they have never seen a human being before – or at least not here – and they come to the conclusion that your story is unbelievable and that you are a spy. Although they all agree that you must be disposed of, they are reluctant fighters, but in the end two of them step forward, drawing their shortswords as they advance. You can fight them one at a time.

	SKILL	STAMINA
First WOOD ELF	8	6
Second WOOD ELF	7	7

Add 1 point to your TRAIL score. If you defeat them both, the two survivors run off into the woods. You ignore them and turn your attention to the captive in the net. Turn to **125**.

151

As soon as you touch one of the coloured switches a shrill bell starts to ring. *'Unauthorized use of transporter!'* the voice in the air shrieks again. *'Transporter settings altered!'* You flick a few more switches, press some illuminated buttons and jump on the platform, which immediately begins to glow. A cloud of light envelops you, but you are able to see one of the room's metallic walls sliding upwards to reveal a nightmarish monster of steel and glass; and then the scene fades as you feel yourself being transported. Roll one die. If you roll:

1	Turn to 105
2	Turn to 115
3	Turn to 126
4	Turn to 135
5	Turn to 145
6	Turn to 234

152

The tunnel ends at a wooden door. Cautiously you pull it open to reveal a small cave which is clearly a store cupboard for the Ophidians' equipment. Spears are stacked against the wall and coils of rope and several suits of glassy black armour hang from hooks. You take down the shortest suit of armour and try it on. Although you manage to fasten the plates of black glass round your limbs and torso you find that your movements are restricted. However, you do discover the secret of the Ophidians' prodigious ability to climb sheer surfaces: the gauntlets of the armour are fitted with retractable metal hooks. If you think Ophidian armour will be useful you can wear it from now on; deduct 1 point from your SKILL because of your hampered movements (and if you have Cerod the Harp you must abandon him here as you cannot carry him while wearing the armour). Whether you wear the armour or not, you can take the set of pipes that hangs from the belt, if you wish. (Record these changes on your *Adventure Sheet*.) You take a coil of rope to the mouth of the cave and tie one end to a boulder, throwing the rest down the escarpment to assist your descent. If you are wearing Ophidian armour you find the rope unnecessary, as the retractable hooks make climbing simple; but whichever way you do it, you reach the foot of the rock face without incident. Restore 1 point of LUCK. You set off towards the vast cliffs that rise from this level of the Ziggurat World to the next. Turn to **4**.

153

You manage to free yourself from the sticky filaments – but too late. Even as you turn to flee, the Spider's mandibles meet in the flesh of your thigh, releasing their venom into your veins. Spurred on by the pain, you dash through the first exit from the courtyard that you can see. It is only as you stagger through the dark tunnels that you begin to feel the effects of the poison: roll one die, add three to the result and deduct the total from your STAMINA. If you are still alive, it is worth finding out where you are going. Roll one die; if the result is:

1	Turn to **15**
2	Turn to **367**
3	Turn to **317**
4	Turn to **285**
5 or 6	Roll again

154

A perfectly aimed throw! The ball flies into the Lithogen's throat and stays there, firmly jammed in place, in spite of the monster's great coughs. You see its luminous eyes widen in shock and outrage – and then they slowly close, as the creature's brain is overcome by the noxious fumes that are emanating from its great stomach and can no longer escape through its throat. You stick your sword into the fleshy tongue to which your feet are stuck: there is no reaction from the Lithogen. You cut yourself free, and continue on your way – turn to **272**.

155

The chariot is pulled by two black horses with red eyes and bronze armour. They are whinnying in confusion, pulling the chariot in circles and trampling the wounded under their hooves. Several Elves fight their way towards you, but they cannot reach the chariot; the wheels, glowing with a pale luminescence, seem to terrify them. You can do nothing but cower in the chariot as the horses career across the moorland. Suddenly a wheel hits a boulder. The axle snaps, you and the broken wheel are thrown clear and the horses drag the wreckage into the distance.

You recover your breath, and inspect the wheel: its luminosity comes from the circular, rune-engraved bronze cover of the hub. The metal roundel is apparently dangerous to Elves, but it causes you no harm. (If you keep it, make a note on your *Adventure Sheet*.) You scan the landscape: you are alone. You take the Aleph

from your pack and lose yourself in studying its myriad moving pictures. It seems to expand and surround you. Roll one die: if you roll an even number, turn to **51**; if you roll an odd number, turn to **36**.

156

You are staring down into a steep-sided gorge. Hundreds of metres below you, in the cleft between the thickly-wooded cliffs, you make out the silver ribbon of a fast-flowing stream. You look up: the cliffs rise above you and on the far side of the gorge, the sky a thin strip of blue between the craggy cliff-tops. You are on a narrow path that meanders precariously along the mid-point of one of the sides of the gorge. You have no choice but to walk – carefully – along it.

You walk for hours. You meet no one, and see no sign of habitation. Dusk is falling, and the bottom of the gorge is already hidden in inky darkness, when you round a bend and see that your way is blocked by a grim fortress. The path ends at a doorway beneath a turretted gatehouse. Approaching cautiously, you see that the castle is derelict and apparently deserted. There are gaps in the battlements, and fallen blocks of stone lie scattered across the path. Then, suddenly, flickering lights spring into life behind the arrow-slits. A moving shape – the silhouette of a child – appears on the battlements and the silence is broken by an eerie scream. If you want to follow the path through the forbidding castle doorway, turn to **391**. If not, you must use the Aleph to take you away – turn to **61**.

157

As you crash through the undergrowth you can hear the music of the harp calling to you. With your hands pressed to your ears, you ignore the brambles that catch your legs and the branches that whip across your face, and eventually the insidious melody fades. You have escaped the Minstrel's enchantment – but now you are lost in the depths of a trackless forest. You have no choice but to use the Aleph to transport you elsewhere. Turn to **91**.

158

You hold the gem between your fingers and slowly raise it before the monster's face. It begins to mewl piteously and edges towards you. You put up no resistance when, with a growl, it lashes out with one of its clumsy, ill-fitted limbs and snatches the jewel from your grasp. It shuffles away from you and drops in a tangle of arms and legs on to its bedding. It only has eyes for its bright new plaything (cross the gem from your *Adventure Sheet*). The hybrid creature does not notice as you leave through the door at the far end of the room. Turn to **258**.

159

As hungry as you are, you dare not risk eating the innkeeper's food. If you have Provisions of your own in your backpack, you can eat a meal and restore up to 4 points of STAMINA. You lie down on the mattress and drift into sleep, lulled by the soft lapping of the river beneath your room. Turn to **195**.

160

Standing squarely in the path of the charging Colepod, you wait until it is almost upon you before aiming your sword-blow at a point above the creature's snapping mandibles and between its waving antennae. *Test your Luck*. If you are Lucky, turn to **374**; if you are Unlucky, turn to **210**.

161

You catch hold of the harness of the leading war-beast and pull yourself clear of the ground, hanging on grimly as the hunt races across the parkland. You are close to the armoured knee of the beast's giant rider and expect him to try to dislodge you from your precarious position, but you look up to find that his face is as unmoving as a statue's. Next to you, hanging by a strap, is the giant's hunting-horn, fashioned from the spiral horn of an animal and decorated with bands of silver. The hunt has spread out now and you can drop to the ground without fear of being trampled. As you release your hold on the harness, you grab the horn. You hit the grass, roll forward, and then jump to your feet to inspect your new acquisition. It looks valuable (note it on your *Adventure Sheet*). If you want to sound the horn, to find out what noise it makes, turn to **209**; if not, you stow it in your backpack and turn to **358**.

162

You choose the path that leads directly towards the Vitreous Citadel. On this route there is just one Silica Serpent between you and your goal. As you approach the monster you see that it is tied, by means of a chain round its neck leading to an iron hoop set into the centre of the path, but it is otherwise free to rend you, bite you and spray you with its acidic venom. It will not be easy to pass this sentry. If you have a set of Ophidian pipes, turn to **288**; if not, turn to **343**.

163

The Logic Dog cannot be defeated. Not only is it stronger and faster than any fighting-dog you have encountered, but if you are skilful enough to strike it, it disappears into the air a second before your blow lands – only to reappear, a second later, behind you. But you cannot escape, so you fight on hopelessly.

LOGIC DOG   SKILL 10

After three Attack Rounds, during which you have been unable to hit the Logic Dog even once, you are becoming resigned – if you are still alive – to the fact that your death is imminent. At that moment a voice calls from above: 'Enough, Logic! Hold back now! Our uninvited visitor has learnt that the garden is well guarded. I will come down and find out what this warrior wants.' The Logic Dog disappears and this time does not reappear. Add 1 point to your TRAIL score, and turn to **282**.

164

You walk for hours between the never-ending book-shelves. In the distance you see a notice, hanging from chains that disappear into the darkness of the ceiling. As you approach, you can make out the words *Lost*

Property and the symbol of a hand pointing downwards. When you reach the notice, you see that in a gap between the bookshelves a narrow staircase descends from the corridor. If you decide to walk down the stairs, turn to **127**. If you decide to continue along the corridor, turn to **373**.

165

The ball misses the Lithogen's throat and hits the creature somewhere below its eyes – on its nose, perhaps, although in the darkness you cannot see whether it actually has one. With a convulsive cough, the Lithogen vomits a second gush of digestive fluid, which begins to eat away your clothing and exposed skin. Lose 2 points of STAMINA. If you are still alive, you have no choice but to try to cut your way out. Turn to **341**.

166

On the dais above you the Elven priest's incantations reach a loud climax. You hear the gurgling rumble of water rushing through old pipes, and a sheet of liquid splashes all round you. The poisoned water soaks through your clothes and into your skin, then you, and Grondel beside you, are screaming in horror as you feel your flesh and muscle begin to disintegrate. Your adventure ends here.

167

The rustling and twittering noises are closing in all round you. Your imagination conjures up all kinds of horrors as you feel scores of fangs nipping your flesh. In this complete darkness, you dare not run, but you must make what speed you can — but in which direction? If you decide to continue onwards into the cave, hoping to stumble across an exit at the far end, turn to **293**; if you turn back, and try to retrace your steps to the door, turn to **244**.

168

Your probing fingers encounter a carving in the centre of the wall that blocks the tunnel. Peering in the dim light you make out a curious figure, something like an abstract representation of a face that is also a small maze (see the diagram). The 'mouth' of the design contains the word *WELCOME*, while each of the two 'eyes' consists of a depression within which there is a button that can be pressed inwards.

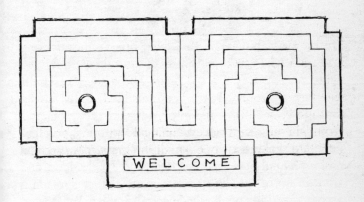

Will you press the button in the right 'eye' (turn to 290), the one in the left 'eye' (turn to 216), or will you do nothing and wait for something to happen (turn to 95)?

169
You spin around to face your next opponent, but the
Feliti are slinking away through the grass, yowling and
casting fearful glances at the dark sky. You look up, and
stare in horror at the ghostly image that is spreading
across the firmament — a Spectral Stalker! Its faceted
eyes glint as it turns its tentacled head this way and
that, tirelessly searching for you and the Aleph. Then,
like smoke in a gust of wind, the image dissolves and
you are alone on the plain once more. Add 1 point to
your TRAIL score, and decide what to do next:
return to the walled garden (turn to **334**); make for the
fortress that you saw from the garden (turn to **379**); or
use the Aleph to take you away from this strange
world (turn to **365**).

You hear the sound of many feet and at first you fear a stampede of Colepods, but the strange beings that canter through the grass to surround you are Mantirs, the owners and shepherds of the Colepod herds. Like a Colepod, a Mantir resembles a giant insect, with a shell-like carapace and antennae waving from his forehead; but he walks upright, on only four legs, his foremost pair of limbs serving as arms. Each Mantir carries a spear and wears headgear as protection from the heat that beats upon the shadeless plains, and each has fashioned the knob of bone at the end of his tail into a spiked weapon of devastating effect. The Mantir herdsmen are as astounded by your appearance as they are impressed by the fact that you have slaughtered their rogue Colepod with a single blow. Their leader addresses you in a fluting voice that you can barely understand. He says that although you are a valiant warrior with whom the Mantir people have no quarrel, nonetheless a Colepod is a valuable beast. As you have killed one of the largest in the herd you must make restitution. If you will not pay for the Colepod, the Mantir says that his tribal law will oblige him to challenge you to a duel. Will you pay the Mantir (turn to **270**) or accept the duel (turn to **223**)?

You are standing in a flat meadow divided by lines of flags into forty-nine squares. Most of the squares are empty, but six contain the bodies of slain warriors. You are holding a long, steel-pointed pike – and you quickly find that you cannot loosen your grip on the weapon. At your back, extending from your heels to the crown of your head, you feel the weight of a plate of iron, held in place by straps across your shoulders, chest and thighs. The front of your body is unprotected: your only garment is a white tunic. You see that four of the bodies are wearing identical tunics; the other two bodies wear black tunics. Apart from you, there are two other surviving warriors in white tunics; they look dispirited and battle-weary. Five warriors in black tunics appear ferocious and jubilant. Each warrior is standing, as you are, in a separate square, and each wears a plate of solid metal on his back.

'You have placed your last pawn, Drawenna,' a male voice booms across the sky, 'and still my forces out-number yours. Are you beginning to regret that you chose this method of resolving our dispute? Soon I will win; and you, and all your lands, will be mine. Resign yourself to it, my soon-to be wife!'

A woman's voice echoes somewhere above the clouds. 'Never, Burud!' she says in a voice quivering with rage. 'I still have a chance to win!'

'You deceive yourself, Drawenna,' the male voice drawls, 'but I will humour you. Let us play on. One of your pawns must move.'

'Do not be impatient, Burud,' the woman's voice replies. 'I have first to teach my latest recruit the rules of battle.' The clouds part and a ray of sunlight illuminates the square that you occupy. Drawenna's voice explains to you the rules of this strange game. Turn to 81.

172

'Stubborn imbecile!' Globus bellows. 'If you will not give me the Aleph, I have the power to take it. Have you forgotten my demonic hunters? I have only to summon the Spectral Stalkers and they will destroy you. Their task done, they will be free; you will be dead and I will have the Aleph. Is that the end you seek? Give me the Aleph, and live.'

You make no reply. Globus continues to plead with you, but at last realizes he has no alternative but to summon his nightmarish servants. He traces a pattern in the air and looks on with trepidation in his face as four hideous shapes begin to materialize. Will you try to break into the Prism of Power by using your weapon (turn to 82); throw the Aleph at the Prism in the hope that the marvellous sphere can counter Globus's power (turn to 268); or will you, at last, agree to the Archmage's demand and pass the Aleph to him through the wall of the Prism (turn to 396)?

173

Metron takes the Hunting-Horn and fixes it into a clamp on a workbench. Many minutes pass while the Mapmaker busies himself with rulers, protractors, tubes of coloured fluids and instruments with flashing lights and glowing numbers. He consults books from his library, draws a diagram of the horn and writes pages of notes. 'An inefficient instrument,' Metron says as he returns the horn to you. 'The basic material is organic, probably from an animal life-form, and very heavy. It measures five and one-eighth *dronks* in length, which is very wasteful — a more consistent tone could be produced from a simpler instrument less than half that size.' You look suspiciously at the horn. It looks unchanged, and yet ... You put it to your lips and blow cautiously. A reedy noise emerges and fades when you stop blowing. The god's Hunting Horn is now no more than an ordinary horn — it has no special powers (cross it from your *Adventure Sheet*). You complain bitterly to the Mapmaker that he has destroyed a magical item. Turn to **375**.

174

After several bone-jolting minutes, the Colepod tosses its head and swerves wildly. You cannot keep your grip and find yourself flying through the air to land heavily on the trampled grass. Lose 2 STAMINA points. If you are still alive, you see the Colepod disappear into the long grass. After recovering your breath, you stand up. Turn to **41**.

175

'Well, sit yourself down!' says Wayland. 'No! Not there! That's the Automatic Impaler. Sit over here. That's right. Now then: what can I be doing for you?'

You unwind the cloth that covers the small ball. Grey

clouds are covering the ever-changing landscapes in the sphere, but Wayland recognizes it instantly — and for several moments he sits open-mouthed in amazement. 'By my hammer and anvil!' he mutters at last. 'And by all the microparticles in the Macrocosmos! It's the Aleph. The one and only sphere of all the spheres! There in your hand, warrior, you hold everything — everything that exists, everywhere. Except here in Limbo, of course. But everything else, everywhere else. Wise men have hunted this object since the birth of the universe. You should take it away from here; the Aleph cannot reside in Limbo. But I beg you, tell me how you came by it.'

If you want to leave the Library in Limbo, Wayland allows you to return to the book-lined corridor — turn to **27**. If you tell Wayland how you received the Aleph, turn to **267**.

The energy you are expending as you fight the Silica Serpent is attracting the attention of your demonic pursuers. Add 1 point to your TRAIL score. The Serpent senses something amiss; its huge black eyes turn this way and that and it shuffles backwards on its myriad legs. You seize your opportunity and deliver it a fatal blow. But as you watch the Serpent's dying convulsions, a shadow darkens the Crystal Garden. You look up. The hideous shape of a Spectral Stalker is forming in the air! As it materializes, its eyes search back and forth, and its tentacles seem to be sensing your scent on the air. *Test your Trail score.* Roll three dice. If the total is equal to, or more than, your TRAIL score, turn to 17; if the total is less than your TRAIL score, turn to 300.

177

You jump from the stage and the crowd parts in front of you. Behind you, the Conjuror is shouting. 'Stop that warrior!' he orders. 'Without the stranger I cannot bring back the Baron's daughter!' With a roar, the crowd turns to pursue you. The Baron's coachman whips his horses and sets off in pursuit too. You are in a small town; old buildings and narrow streets surround you. Hounded by the mob, and increasingly desperate (add 1 point to your TRAIL score), you race across the cobbles and double-back along dark alleys. At last you manage to put some distance between yourself and your pursuers and you find yourself back in the town square. The Conjuror's wagon is in front of you and Felice is holding the reins and urging on the team of black stallions. If you want to run and jump on to the back of the wagon, turn to 24. Otherwise, with the sounds of pursuit approaching, you have no choice but to use the Aleph to leave this place and go elsewhere — turn to 63.

178

You cannot hope to win this fight but you know that you can expect no mercy from the Black Shadows. Soon a pile of black corpses lies at your feet, but they have inexhaustible reinforcements, while your STAMINA is all too finite, and you are engulfed by a wall of flapping, leathery bodies. If you have more than 4 points of STAMINA, you manage to keep struggling for a while; but eventually your STAMINA is reduced to 4 and you begin to falter. Then – add 1 point to your TRAIL score – the Black Shadows begin to screech in fear, and back away from you. As they fall back you see the hideous shape of a Spectral Stalker forming in the air. As it materializes its eyes search back and forth, and its writhing mass of tentacles seems to be sensing your scent on the air. *Test your Trail score.* Roll three dice. If the total is equal to, or greater than, your TRAIL score, turn to **7**; if the total is less than your TRAIL score, turn to **300**.

179

Semeion gazes perplexedly at the objects on the table. 'These signs have a meaning,' he says at last, 'but all they tell *me* is that the Spectral Stalkers have been summoned and set on a quest by a powerful and evil sorcerer. We could have guessed as much. I can advise you only to be on your guard against wizards – and I am sure you do not need me to tell you that!'

'Globus is presumably a wizard of some sort,' you reply. 'Can you tell me more about him?' Semeion readily agrees to try. Turn to **308**.

180

Sand dunes stretch in every direction. Scrubby bushes grow in the hollows, tough grass waves in clumps on the rounded summits. At the edge of a distant pool of water stands a village; the huts, on wooden stilts, are made of reeds and leaves. On the edge of the village you pass through an abandoned market, its rickety stalls empty and covered with dust. Then you see that one stall is still in use: only a few items are on display, but they are quite remarkable. They look like roughly-made candles, apparently formed out of clay, but each has a tip that glows brightly enough to be visible in full daylight. The old woman behind the stall begs you to buy one; and if you have a Gold Piece to spare, you may do so. (Record the transaction on your *Adventure Sheet*.) She tells you that these few Glowcandles are all that remains of her village's wealth and possessions. Mayrek the Potter, the hermit who makes the Glow-candles and other wonderful things, has not been seen for months. Men from the village have gone to look for him – but they have not returned. Will you go to the village and offer to help the villagers (turn to **66**)? Or will you turn away and set off across the dunes in the opposite direction (turn to **117**)?

181

You pull the Heatsword from its scabbard and apply the blade to the folds of fungus. The sword looks just like an ordinary weapon but the blade must be as hot as a furnace, for the fungus blackens and shrivels all round it. Soon you can see wooden panels behind the smould-ering fungus and within minutes you think you will be able to clear the whole door. However, you are becom-ing engulfed in the clouds of black smoke given off by the incinerated fungus. You cannot breathe; you stagger and fall to your knees. Your only hope is to find a way through the door before the smoke poisons you. Roll four dice. If the total is less than, or equal to, your

STAMINA, turn to **274**; if the total is more than your STAMINA, turn to **90**.

182

'A weapon?' Semeion asks in astonishment. 'I am a reader of signs, not an armourer. But let me think – I had a visitor once, long ago, who left a sword behind when he left. I will see if I can find it.' You wait in the garden for a long time, listening to crashes and thumps come from all sides of the courtyard as Semeion searches every room. At last he emerges carrying a plain sword in a scabbard. 'Found it!' he says. 'It's a very ordinary sword, as far as I can tell. But if you think it will help you, by all means take it.' If you have no weapon you can take the sword and restore 2 points of SKILL. You then decide that you must take your leave of Semeion and, gazing into the Aleph, you allow yourself to become lost within its teeming worlds. Turn to **234**.

183

Lying in the grass at your feet is a large Hunting-Horn, fashioned from the spiral horn of an animal and decorated with silver bands. You must have pulled it from the harness of the leading war-beast. It is an impressive item, and looks valuable (if you decide to keep it, record it on your *Adventure Sheet*). If you want to sound the horn, turn to **209**; if not, you stow it in your backpack and turn to **358**.

184

As you approach the Silica Serpent you see that the creature has become entangled in a web of fine wires that seems to have been set in the gulley for this very purpose. The creature's desperate contortions are winding the wires ever more tightly about its long, glittering body. It is so preoccupied that it fails to notice you until you are only a few paces away. The Serpent stops moving. You see yourself reflected in its huge black eyes. Then its head darts forward and it spits a jet of liquid at you. Roll two dice: if the total is less than your SKILL, turn to **94**; if the total is equal to or more than your SKILL, turn to **240**.

185

On the other side of the doorway you stumble down a step and into a vaulted corridor. At the other end is a doorway identical to the one you have just stepped through. A counter runs along one side of the corridor, and behind it is a room containing rows of empty hatstands. Asleep on the counter is an old Dwarf. He opens one eye as you approach.

'Good day, I suppose,' he grumbles. 'And I hope you had a fruitful visit to the Library in Limbo. Don't bother to tell me, I don't really care. If you left a cloak or a hat on your way in, don't try asking me for it. This is the way out, and I haven't got anything of anybody's. There's the door from Nowhere to Somewhere.'

'But to where, exactly?' you ask.

'Exactly anywhere you like. Of course, if you want to go somewhere particular, it helps to think about it while you're walking through the door.'

You stride to the doorway and step across the thresh-

old. Do you fill your mind with thoughts of your home world, Khul (turn to **51**); do you try to imagine the Ziggurat World (turn to **234**); or do you think about your mysterious burden, the Aleph, and rely on its influence to choose your destination (turn to **21**)?

186

After only a few minutes of following the twists and turns of this passage, you realize that it is unlike any that you have so far encountered in the maze. For one thing, it seems to be sloping downwards; for another, it is completely dark – there is not a single crack of light to be seen. Feeling your way with outstretched hands, you grope round yet another corner – and almost cry out in fear as you come face to face with a glowing skeleton. It stands in front of you, barring the tunnel with the spear it clutches in its bony hands. It is dressed as a warrior and you wonder whether it is the ghost of an adventurer who died while lost in the maze. Apart from the occasional shake of its spear, it makes no move against you. You decide to step forward, but as soon as you move the skeleton speaks, in a slurred monotone. 'Come not this way!' it orders. 'This way danger lies, and certain death. Turn back! Begone!'

Will you turn back (turn to **257**), or will you advance towards the skeleton (turn to **385**)?

187

You step over a threshold and find yourself in a small chamber with a doorway in each of its four walls. One, as usual, is marked with the circle and triangle symbol.

The doorway opposite it is marked with an arrow pointing downwards; through this doorway you can see a stairway leading down into the ground. You face the usual symbol and decide which doorway to take:

The door before you	Turn to **224**
The door behind you	Turn to **297**
The door to your right	Turn to **329**
The door to your left	Turn to **26**

188

Squatting beside the path, you pick up a small pebble and tap the clay ball. Nothing happens. You tap harder and the ball disintegrates into tiny fragments of baked clay. You search among the pieces for the object that was inside the ball, but you find nothing except for a handful of grey dust, which is soon blown away by the breeze. You sense that you have lost something of the utmost importance; lose 1 point of LUCK. You look around at the hills and the landscape of dunes below. There seems to be no choice but to use the Aleph to leave this place. Turn to **211**.

189

You are in the entrance hall of the Vitreous Citadel. You stand and stare in confused wonderment at the cavernous chamber which, with mirrored walls and burnished ceiling, seems to extend into infinite distance in all directions. Through one of the many doorways you see the strange turquoise sky of the Ziggurat World, and you assume that if you walk through a doorway that leads in the opposite direction you will reach the centre of the Citadel. You set off along corridors of marble and glass whose only inhabitants are angular crystal statues, and at last you reach a circular antechamber. Facing you are two doorways. Beyond one all is darkness; through the other, you can see the edge of a huge, semi-transparent cube bathed in dim green light. Will you go through the dark doorway (turn to **118**), or into the room containing the huge cube (turn to **302**)?

190

You walk towards the cliffs for hours, but they seem to draw no closer. However, the terrain is much hillier now and covered with trees. You head for an isolated peak that is higher than the other hills and, when you reach the summit, proceed to climb up into the branches of a tall tree. From this position you have a panoramic view of the landscape. Behind you is the wall of cliffs, its foot still some distance away. To your right, the hills drop suddenly to a sandy coastline, beyond which an expanse of water stretches to the horizon. In front of you are the woods through which you have been walking. And to your left the woodland clears, and beyond the trees you can see a vast extent of grassy plains. You can see no way of ascending the cliff-face; therefore, to explore new territory you will have to walk towards the water (turn to **92**) or towards the plains (turn to **116**). Alternatively, you may use the Aleph to take you elsewhere (turn to **2**).

191

Grasping the arrow-shaft with both hands, you brace your feet against Syzuk's ribcage and pull with all your might. The arrow springs from the warlord's shoulder-joint and you fall on to your back. Syzuk picks up his sword and gives you a ghastly grin. 'Thank you, fool!' he snarls. 'Your act of kindness will not save you. Now nothing can save my enemies on this battlefield. On, my warriors! Destroy them all! Let none live! We will perform Glund's sacrificial ritual at the summit of a mountain of corpses!' Your only chance is to attack Syzuk while he is still weak from his wound. You launch yourself at his back.

SYZUK   SKILL 8   STAMINA 10

If you defeat him, you hear a chorus of despairing cries from the ranks of Skeletal Warriors. The battle becomes fiercer as their opponents counter-attack and the chariot is caught in a ferocious skirmish. You kick Syzuk's body out of it and try to control the war-horses. Turn to **155**.

192

You lift the trapdoor and lead the way into the gloomy interior of the tower. The room below the turret is unguarded and contains the belongings of the captives – including their weapons. Armed with Elven bows, Vaskind swords and Mantir spears, your little army makes short work of the few Black Shadows it meets as you lead it down through the chambers of the tower. At last you reach the base of the tower. There are only two exits from the vaulted crypt, a door which leads to the outside and a trapdoor in the floor that must lead to cellars – or perhaps an underground passage. The Elves, Mantirs and Vaskind are desperate to return home and are determined to leave the tower through the door to the outside. Will you accompany them (turn to 333), or will you bid them farewell, and set off alone through the trapdoor (turn to 140)?

193

Barogkaz stops fighting and stares upwards in amazement and fear. The hideous shape of a Spectral Stalker is forming in the air above the courtyard. The Zwinian flees, and you run in the opposite direction, seeking shelter from the questing eyes of the Spectral Stalker. You crouch in the doorway of a tower and decide that you have to use the Aleph to escape. Turn to 91.

194

Your head pounds, your chest seems about to burst and your limbs are numb with cold. As you feel yourself slipping into unconsciousness, you clamp a hand over your face in an attempt to prevent yourself drawing sea water into your lungs, and pray that you will drift to the surface of the sea before you pass out. Little by little, as the murky waters around you become lighter, the precious air trickles from your lips. You suck in a gulp of water and in that instant you know you must drown – and then your head breaks through the waves! Coughing and spluttering, you drag yourself on to the beach. You lie there for several minutes, recovering your breath, but no one comes. You decide, at last, to climb the path that zig-zags up the face of the cliff. Turn to 12.

195

You wake up. Everything is dark: the candle has blown out and there is no hint of daylight in the chinks of the shutters. A cold wind, carrying with it the smell of the river, makes you shiver and you sit up. Then you see them. A pair of luminous eyes is staring at you from the middle of the floor. You remember the name of the inn: the Ghostly Visitors. Are you being watched by a ghost? For several seconds you remain as still as the watching eyes; but you have to decide what to do. Will you throw yourself at the intruder, whatever it is (turn to 271)? Or will you keep still and watch silently (turn to 344)?

196

The tunnel spirals downwards becoming ever steeper, until you can no longer keep your footing. A foul stench assails your nostrils as you slide helplessly into a pit of tiny, squirming bodies. You have no way of knowing that you have fallen into a Shadowlings hatchery; but you are soon aware that the little creatures have an insatiable appetite for blood. You cannot escape.

197

Stepping backwards, you speak hurriedly as the Logic Dog advances on you. 'You're wrong,' you tell the dog. 'I guessed that you would attack me. If you attack me now, that will prove that I guessed correctly. And you promised that if I guessed correctly, you would let me pass. Therefore, now that you have announced that you are going to attack, you must let me pass.'

The Logic Dog stops in its tracks and its two heads turn to regard each other with dazed expressions. After a few moments of thought, both heads let out a howl of frustration – and the Dog disappears. A voice hails you from above: 'Bravo, stranger! You have done well: not only have you found the path through my labyrinth, but you have also defeated my faithful Logic Dog with its own weapon. I will come down and greet you.' Turn to **282**.

198

The knocker raps loudly on the heavy wooden door. You wait for a reply; nothing happens but the sudden appearance of a light behind the little glass circle. Then, in a gravelly voice, the door itself speaks to you! 'You are a human warrior. You possess eight coins of gold. Please insert four coins into the slot and enter.'

Will you follow these instructions and put 4 Gold Pieces into the slot in the door, before going through the doorway (turn to **147**)? Will you ignore the voice and push open the door immediately (turn to **286**)? Or will you abandon the idea of going through this door, and instead look for a way out of the Library (turn to **27**)?

199

The door swings inwards when you push it. You peer into the tower and see, beyond the short corridor formed by the thickness of the wall, a small, dark and apparently empty chamber. You step forward into the room and are startled by a crash from behind you. You barely have time to realize that a portcullis has descended to block your exit, however, because you are attacked by the creatures that were roosting near the ceiling. You have no more than a fleeting impression of black membranous wings, malevolent red eyes and cruelly-curved talons. You feel a brief pang of pain as sharp teeth penetrate your flesh; then the creatures' venom starts to work, and you drift into unconsciousness. Turn to **291**.

200

You stand underneath the dangling bundle. It is larger than a man and seems to be a sort of cocoon of sticky fibres. It twitches suddenly and then speaks. 'Is — is there anybody there? Anybody? Please, if you can, help me out of this thing! I'm trapped, I can't escape! I've been here for months! Please help me!'

Will you try to release whoever is inside the cocoon? If so, turn to **339**. If you would rather leave this room, turn to **45**.

201

The door flies open, revealing a cupboard packed with stores. There is no room for you to hide inside so you start inspecting the contents of the shelves for anything that might be a weapon. All of the items are unfamiliar to you: they are made of unnaturally smooth materials, and most are either completely featureless or covered in indecipherable symbols. One object, however, looks like it might be a weapon: it has a hand-grip, a trigger and a tube, ending in a nozzle, that can be aimed. It is clearly labelled *Extinguisher*, which sounds to you like an eminently suitable name for a weapon. You are about to test its power when you hear the sound of heavy footsteps approaching. Will you wait for whatever is about to confront you (turn to **96**)? Alternatively, you could throw some of the switches on the central console and leap on to the platform in the hope that you will be taken elsewhere (turn to **151**).

202

You push open the door, and step into utter blackness; it closes behind you. You hear the echo of your footsteps, suggesting that you are in a large hall or cavern; and then you hear other noises – a gradual crescendo of twittering, rustling and squeaking. You take a few more steps forward, wondering whether you have entered a cave full of bats. Something brushes against your body. Teeth nip your ankle and you jerk your foot away. The darkness is oppressive; if you have a source of light – a Glowcandle, a Colepod Lantern or a Ring of Light – you can use it to illuminate your surroundings; turn to **351**. If you have no means of creating light, turn to **167**.

203

As clouds of darkness roll over your mind, your last thought is that you are dying, but you recover your senses to find that Semeion has torn the Energy Leech from your arm. You are weak and nauseous and you have only 1 point of STAMINA, but you are alive. You are too exhausted to make another attempt to penetrate the sorcerous defences within which Globus has cloaked his citadel. Instead, you weakly agree to Semeion's suggestion that you should try to use the Telopticon to see the Spectral Stalkers. Turn to **380**.

204

You retrieve the bottle of Siccator from your backpack and uncork it. You assume that if water makes the Golem fast and strong, the drying effect of the Siccator will slow the monster. But first you have to succeed in sprinkling the liquid over its body. You know you will have only one chance. You stand ready, feeling the ground shake under your feet as the Golem pounds towards you, swinging its mallet. Roll two dice. If the total is less than your SKILL score, turn to **337**. If the total is equal to, or higher than, your SKILL score, turn to **141**.

205

No matter how much you struggle you cannot escape. Eventually, like the other prisoners, you simply hang limply in your bonds, your head drooping and your limbs numb. The sound of loud flapping alerts you to the return of the Black Shadows. Without pausing to perch on the parapet the slavering creatures fly straight into the belvedere, their red eyes glinting greedily as they cluster round the writhing, moaning prisoners. You watch in horror as the loathsome creatures begin to flap towards you. Soon you are overwhelmed by overlapping blankets of foetid blackness, and you feel venomous fangs piercing your flesh. As your blood is sucked from your body you weaken – reduce your STAMINA to 2 points – and the venom begins to work. You are dimly aware of being untied, your pack being strapped to your back and of being carried sky-wards; then you lose consciousness. Turn to **392**.

206

You trudge for what seems like endless hours along a rocky passage, until you feel weak from exhaustion. Deduct one point of STAMINA. At last you see a glimmer of light ahead, and you turn a corner to find yourself in a square courtyard with a flagstone floor. The dim light that filters down the shaft formed by the sheer walls of the courtyard is dimmed by a vast web that is floating down the shaft, and long strands of it are almost touching you. From the web a gigantic Spider begins to scuttle down a silvery thread. One of the strands touches you and sticks to your clothing. Within seconds you are struggling to free yourself from a mass of finger-thick filaments. Roll two dice. If the total is less than your SKILL, turn to **69**; if the

total is equal to, or more than, your SKILL, turn to
153.

207

The wind howls around you with renewed fury as you
make for the protection of the trees. Something makes
you look back and you see a disturbance in the air
above the body of the creature that fell out of the sky.
A dark figure, twice as tall as a man, is solidifying out
of the air as you watch. Its outline is still indistinct, but
it is moving, twisting and turning, as if searching the
landscape.

Will you stand and watch it arrive (turn to **129**), or will
you run to find a hiding-place in the edge of the forest
(turn to **44**)?

208

Holding the Umbrella before you like a shield, you
crouch low and charge into the midst of the glass
flowers, striking to right and left as you run. The air is
filled with the sound of splintering glass and the shrieks
released by the flowers as they are cut down; but there
are many more blooms that remain, on all sides of you,
squirting acid from within their petals. Roll two dice. If
the total is greater than your SKILL, you are wounded
by the flowers' corrosive spray; the difference between
the two figures is the number of STAMINA points
you lose. If you survive, you emerge on the other side
of the flower bed holding an Umbrella that is no more
than a smoking framework of wire (delete it from your

Adventure Sheet), but you are able to continue towards the Vitreous Citadel. Turn to **336**.

209

You put the Hunting-Horn to your lips and blow. A deep note, like the bellow of a bull, issues forth. What's more, when you stop blowing the sound continues – and begins to swell! The noise is deafening; the ground itself is resonating with the deep tone of the Horn. The war-beasts rear and buck in confusion and their gigantic riders, shaken from their indifference at last, turn in their saddles to stare at you in amazement. Struggling to keep your balance as the ground vibrates, you see in the distance a group of nymphs and satyrs, the prey of the hunt, jumping with glee at the giants' discomfiture. You fear that this disturbance will attract the attention of those that are hunting you – add 1 point to your TRAIL score. The faces of the giants continue to display outrage as they fade, become transparent, and disappear from the park. At last the sound of the Horn begins to diminish. As the noise quietens, the landscape around you darkens, and you feel yourself falling into a pit of blackness. You blink your eyes and find yourself in a cave, standing within a circle of fires. Also within the circle is an old crone, who watches you silently. Will you attack her (turn to **273**), or question her (turn to **314**)?

210

Your sword plunges into the Colepod and remains fixed there, jammed between two scaly plates. The creature rears in pain and your sword is snatched from your hand. The wounded and maddened Colepod races away into the grass. If you have no other weapon you must reduce your SKILL by 2 points when in combat, until you acquire another one. Turn to **41**.

211

Pulling the Aleph from your backpack, you hold it between your hands. You stare wonderingly into its infinite depths, entranced by the ever-changing visions that swarm before your eyes. Strange creatures, alien peoples, towns, continents, planets and swirling stars meet your gaze wherever you look. Roll one die. If you roll an even number, turn to **105**; if you roll an odd number, turn to **248**.

212

Only your will-power keeps you clinging to life. The brilliant beam of light will crush you like an insect at any moment. Then the light flickers and begins to fade. Suddenly you are free; you have survived the onslaught. You are once again alone in the dim light of the long hallway. Turn to **386**.

Having passed the forest guards and the watch-tower, the Minstrel is not challenged again, even at the gate of the citadel. Within the walls the streets are decked with flags; the taverns are full of boar-faced Zwinians making merry. You and the Minstrel attract stares but a few notes from the Minstrel's harp ensure a hearty welcome. You ask the Minstrel about the celebrations. 'It is seven years to the day since I was banished,' he replies. 'No doubt the usurper Frampa has declared a day of revelling. He will rue it.'

The Minstrel leads you up to the inner bailey of the Keep where the court, in finest robes, are seated at a banquet watched by a throng of townspeople. Frampa, Lord of the Citadel, calls for entertainment. His jester speaks up: 'There is talk of a stranger in the town, sire,' he shouts for the benefit of the whole assembly. 'Call forth the minstrel!'

Frampa, snout gaping in shock, clutches the arms of his throne. 'No!' he yells. 'It is Barogkaz in disguise! The seers warned of a minstrel! Do not let him play!' But it is too late. Wary of your sword, the guards dare not approach the Minstrel as his harp begins to play. The crowd, the courtiers and the guards are struck dumb. Then, as the Minstrel wrests different tunes from the harp, the Zwinians start to laugh uncontrollably and the Minstrel mocks their helpless mirth. He makes them weep, then stand up and dance like marionettes. You are beginning to find the situation threatening; will you continue to watch the Minstrel's tricks (turn to 119), or will you try to stop him (turn to 8)?

You keep to the shadows, scrambling up and down gulleys and stumbling along dark ravines. In a channel between two walls of rock you stub your feet against upthrust pointed boulders. You step over them — and your feet are stuck to the ground. Two round eyes suddenly appear before you. You have stumbled into the extended jaw of a Lithogen, a huge predator that, once adult, never moves; it merely lies in wait for incautious animals. A Lithogen has only a small throat, and cannot eat solid matter; its prey has to be pre-digested and it remains stuck to the Lithogen's tongue, in the lower jaw, until it has rotted down to a pulp that the Lithogen can ingest. To assist the rotting process, the Lithogen's funnel-shaped throat squirts a caustic liquid on to the trapped prey. The first foul-smelling spray catches you unawares, and burns where it splashes your exposed flesh; lose 1 point of STAMINA. You cannot pull your feet free, so you will have to cut yourself free with your sword. Then it occurs to you that with a well-aimed throw you could close the creature's throat — a ball would completely block the funnel-shaped orifice. The Aleph would be the right size . . . but no, you cannot afford to lose it here. If you have a spherical map, however, and want to try to use it for this purpose, turn to **281**; otherwise, you will have to try to cut through the Lithogen's tongue — turn to **341**.

215

Your head feels like an overripe melon and your body is being shaken like a sapling in a gale. You come to your senses and realize that you are lying on the floor of a moving vehicle. You open your eyes: towering above you is Syzuk the Devastator, his eye-sockets blazing like beacons as he cracks a whip in one bony hand and brandishes a flaming longsword in the other. You are in his war-chariot, in the thick of a bloody battle. The day is Syzuk's: his Skeletal Warriors, marching forward in endless ranks, cover the land like a flood. Like storm-battered islands, small bands of Syzuk's enemies – humans, mainly, and some Elves – die fighting to hold back the tide. A solitary, desperate Elven arrow arcs across the sky and lands in Syzuk's shoulder. He falls alongside you. The Elven arrowhead is poison to him and he pleads with you to help him. If you decide to do so, and you have a bottle of Corrective Fluid, turn to **384**. If you want to help but have no Fluid, turn to **191**. If you finish off Syzuk and bundle him out of the chariot, turn to **155**.

216

You press the button on the left-hand side of the design and the wall starts to move. The huge slab of rock rises slowly to reveal another square courtyard, but this one is much larger than any you have encountered in the maze so far. It is a garden, the lawns and trees separated by paths that appear as Labyrinthine as the tunnels of the maze. The four sheer walls are covered, as far upwards as you can see, with balconies, windows and belvederes, all of them interconnected by stairways and ramps that baffle your sight and defy comprehension. Standing in front of you, its muscles quivering with suppressed energy, is a gigantic two-headed dog. You prepare to defend yourself, for the creature is clearly ready to pounce; but instead, from both of its fang-filled mouths, it speaks.

'I am the Logic Dog,' it growls, 'and my task is to protect the garden of my master Semeion from intruders. I could attack you; or I could let you pass. Which do you think I will do? Will I attack, or will I let you pass? For you see, if you guess correctly, I will let you pass; but if you guess wrongly, I will attack.' Will you tell the Logic Dog that you think it will attack you (turn to 320); or will you guess that the Dog will let you pass (turn to 72)?

217

You pull the glowing sphere from your backpack and cup it in your hands. Instantly you are mesmerized by the myriad visions, so tiny and yet so detailed, that swarm within the Aleph. The longer you gaze, the more you can see: strange creatures, alien peoples, towns, continents, planets, swirling stars. You feel yourself being enveloped by the Aleph; but what thoughts pass through your mind as you are transported? If you are anxious to find someone who can explain the meaning of the objects that you have collected since you were given the Aleph, turn to 354. If you are keen to continue on your travels, hoping to find more significant items of booty, turn to 156. If, however, your only concern is to hurry on to the end of your quest, turn to 234.

218

Stones crumble beneath your feet, your fingernails splinter against barely-accessible handholds and a hundred times you think you are about to plummet to your death. But at last you pull yourself over a lip of rock and find yourself at the entrance of a cave. The Ophidians, confident that they alone of unwinged creatures can reach this eyrie, have left the place unguarded. You are able to rest undisturbed until your limbs stop shaking and your muscles no longer ache. You peer into the cave: two tunnels lead away into the darkness. From the one to your left you hear the shrieks of Silica Serpents, and see leaping shadows cast by fires; the tunnel to your right is silent, but illuminated by torches in brackets set into the wall. Will you explore the left tunnel (turn to 43), or the right (turn to 152)?

219

You offer no resistance as the Feliti converge on you, their fangs bared. The pack surrounds you, the largest of the creatures at your heels. They nip your legs to encourage you to move and despite your exhaustion you force yourself to run. You are in a sea of green bodies surging across the evening landscape. When you stagger, you are bitten; when you fall, your limbs are grasped between fang-filled jaws and you are dragged across the rocks until you pull yourself upright. When you trip and fall for the third time you are too tired and battered to bother about your fate. You lie on the hard ground and wait to be torn apart — but nothing happens. You lift your head: the Feliti are running on without you, disappearing into the darkness towards the garden. Night has fallen. You have lost 4 points of STAMINA. You manage to stand; where will you go now: back to the garden (turn to **334**), towards the fortress that you saw from the garden (turn to **379**), or will you use the Aleph to escape from this strange world (turn to **365**)?

back to the garden (turn to **334**), towards the fortress that you saw from the garden (turn to **379**), or will you use the Aleph to escape from this strange world (turn to **365**)?

220

Semeion gazes perplexedly at the objects on the table. 'These signs contain a meaning,' he says at last, 'but it is difficult to read. They seem to suggest that the Spectral Stalkers have been summoned by Globus, but I cannot tell for what purpose. Perhaps they escaped his control and are pursuing the Aleph because it calls to them. Perhaps Globus was over-eager to recover the Aleph and unleashed the Stalkers by mistake. Or maybe he is not the Aleph's rightful owner, and has summoned the Stalkers to find it for him. I cannot tell. But it would be unwise to trust Globus, I think. Be on your guard.'

You thank Semeion for this rather superfluous advice and ask if he can tell you more about Globus. Turn to 308.

221

Holding your breath at every step, you climb upwards. You reach the eighteenth step without feeling the slightest tremor. With great care, you leap over the nineteenth without touching it and land on the twentieth step — where an electric charge as powerful as a bolt of lightning fries you in an instant! The adventure ends here for warriors who fail to calculate correctly.

222

You duck through the low doorway and enter the inn. A gust of wind slams the door behind you. In the darkness you can just make out tables and chairs; the room seems to be deserted and there is no sound to be heard. You climb a staircase until you reach a landing lit by a candle. There are several doors; all but one are locked. You open the unlocked door and find yourself in a pleasant bedroom with a balcony overhanging the river. Clean blankets have been laid on the rush mattress and there is a basin of fresh water. Supper is waiting on the table: bread, cold meat, cheese and a flagon of ale. The food looks wholesome; will you eat it (turn to 113), or are you too suspicious to try it (turn to 159)?

223

A Mantir duel is not a fight to the death. The two combatants are armed with spears, which have to be used only as staves. One of the Mantirs gives you his

spear. The object is to knock your opponent to the
ground; in this the Mantir has an advantage over a
human opponent, because he stands on four legs and
has an additional weapon — the spiked ball on the end
of his tail. Because of this, the Mantir attacks twice in
each Attack Round, but you can strike him only in the
first of the two attacks — if your Attack Strength is
higher than his in the second attack, this merely indicates that you have avoided the swipe of his bristling
tail. The duel ends when one of you has lost 4 or more
STAMINA points.

MANTIR   SKILL 8   STAMINA 10

If you survive the duel, you realize that the Mantirs
have lost all interest in the result of the contest between
you and their leader. They are staring into the sky and
shrieking in alarm — turn to **388**.

224

Wearily you trudge along the seemingly endless passage. At last you see a patch of light ahead and step
through a portal at the end of the passage into a square
courtyard. The flagstones are littered with pebbles and
small boulders, and only a little grey light seeps into
the courtyard. You suspect that the shaft above you
has been partially blocked by a rockfall. You stand in
the centre of the floor, facing the one doorway which
has the circle and triangle symbol above it, and ponder
which way you should go next. A noise disturbs you
and, looking down, you see that the stones on the floor
are beginning to vibrate. You decide to leave quickly;
but even as you take your first step, some of the stones

start to explode. Sharp shards of flint fly across the courtyard, lacerating your legs as you run. You must reach the shelter of a doorway quickly, or you will be cut down and stoned to death. Roll two dice; if the total is more than your SKILL, you do not reach a haven unscathed — deduct the difference between the two scores from your STAMINA. If you are still alive, you hobble through the doorway you have chosen; did you make for the one you were facing (turn to **26**), the one behind you (turn to **329**), the one to your right (turn to **247**), or the one to your left (turn to **187**)?

'I'm not interested in weapons,' intones the Robot. 'I've got more swords than I know what to do with. Money's no use to me, either. What else have you got?' You bring out your two portions of Provisions; and, with some reluctance, you uncover the small sphere, its surface now dull and cloudy. The Robot merely glances at it. 'So you're the bearer of the Aleph,' he says. 'You'll find there's powerful people searching for that. Food — that's of interest. Not for myself, of course — never touch the stuff — but for my hungry little pets.'

If you have lost your sword, the Robot gives you a replacement; deduct one portion of your Provisions and restore your SKILL to its *Initial* value. He also produces a glass disc with a handle and one of the hanging constructions of wire and cloth; he calls them a Magnifying Glass and an Umbrella and explains how they work. He will exchange them for one portion of Provisions each. You then ask the Robot how you can

leave the Library, and he points to the *EXIT* doorway.
You step through it. Turn to **185**.

226

'Wrong!' roars the doorway. 'Utterly wrong! Why,
foolish intruder, you have only to look at the beautiful
and intricately-worked carvings that adorn the apex of
my framework! There you will see my crowns. Regard
them now: this will be the last sight your eyes will see!'
Turn to **31**.

227

The picture moves closer, until the image of the Spectral
Stalkers fills the Telopticon's metal hoop. The aura that
surrounds the nightmarish creatures seems to be
moving, as if it were being tugged and prodded.
Semeion's mental energy is reaching out to touch the
very stuff of the spell that binds the Stalkers. *This is a
potent enchantment*, Semeion's thoughts interrupt yours.
*It took many minutes to cast, and will take longer to undo.
Charms have been woven into it to ensure that only he who
made the spell can unmake it. Apart from the spellmaker
unmaking the spell, the only way it can be ended is by
fulfilling its purpose: the Spectral Stalkers must destroy the
bearer of the Aleph and carry the Aleph to the spellmaker.
Only then will they be free to return to the unknown plane
whence they came.* As one the Spectral Stalkers turn their
vast heads, and you feel their hate-filled yearning reaching out to you. They have detected you: add 2 points
to your TRAIL score. *In my opinion*, Semeion's
thoughts flash through your mind, *it's time you were on*

your way! He pulls the helmet from your head and hurries you from the chamber. Turn to **23**.

228

One of the black warriors moves to the white end of the field. The white warrior on square *G6* is surrounded and killed by the combined attacks of the three black warriors around him. Burud has won. The sky echoes with his harsh laughter, and you can also hear Drawenna's sobs of despair. You find that you can at last release your hold on the pike and the heavy armour slips from your back. You wander to the edge of the field, where you find your backpack and your clothes. Soon you are ready to depart, and you decide to use the Aleph to travel elsewhere. Turn to **124**.

229

You crouch behind a boulder and watch the struggles of the trapped Silica Serpent. After a while, a band of strange soldiers arrives. They are humanoid but very tall and thin, with long spidery arms and legs, and they are encased in gleaming armour of black glass. Each carries a spear and has a set of pipes hanging at his belt. They are Ophidians and, as they demonstrate, they have the skill to control Silica Serpents.

They surround the Serpent which, although trapped, is not harmless: it spits jets of liquid at the Ophidians, and the liquid is clearly corrosive, as the rocks on which it splashes begin to crumble and smoke. The acid has no effect on the Ophidians, however; it runs off their glass armour, and they pay almost no attention to the creature's angry splutters. Instead, one of them takes the pipes from his belt and begins to play upon them. There is no recognizable tune, but the Silica Serpent seems to find the music very relaxing. It stops spitting and struggling, and the Ophidians move in to muzzle its scaly jaws, bind up its diaphanous wings and lead it away on a leash. If you want to follow them, turn to 369; if you would rather wait until they are out of sight, and then continue along the path to the distant cliff, turn to 4.

230

You walk along the shore, allowing the cool water to lap over your tired feet. If you need to drink sea water to restore STAMINA drained by an Energy Leech, you can do so now. You notice that the damp sand is covered with the tracks of large webbed feet. You pray that the creatures who made the tracks have now gone elsewhere; but when you turn round you come face to face with them. Standing inside a huge bubble that seems to have just emerged from the sea are six amphibious beings. They are man-sized, but look more like giant frogs than humans. From wide, lipless, tooth-filled mouths their long tongues flicker threateningly. They wear necklaces made of shells and coral, and carry swords edged with sharks' teeth. They are Vaskind. The bubble dissolves, and the creatures advance with raised swords. Will you surrender (turn to 261) or defend yourself (turn to 104)?

The Conjuror snarls as you produce the silver blade. This weapon can harm him; he will have to fight you.

VAMPIRE   SKILL 9   STAMINA 13

If you win, a large bat flies from the Vampire's corpse, which then crumbles to dust. In the dust is the key to the hanging cage. You release the Baron's daughter and, despite her urging, you decide not to tackle the Were-cat who is driving the wagon. Instead you open the door, grab your backpack in one hand and the girl's wrist in the other, and jump from the wagon.

You crawl into the shade of a hedge to inspect your pack. Amazingly, nothing is broken — restore 1 point of LUCK — and you find that you have collected one of the Conjuror's circular calling-cards. It displays the words *Marvip the Magician* above a picture of a tall figure with a black cloak and a glowing wand. The shape of the card reminds you of the Aleph and you decide to keep it.

The Baron's daughter has been watching you for some time. 'Are you going to sit there all day?' she complains. 'That Magician was much more exciting than you. He was going to take me to his castle. Now I suppose I'll have to go home to boring old Daddy. Goodbye and good riddance!' With that she strides off towards the town. You decide to use the Aleph to go elsewhere. Turn to **63**.

232

You step tentatively on to the bridge. The stone slab is firm and stable. You take a few more steps — and the slab begins to move. Like a tongue withdrawing into a mouth, the bridge is being pulled into the doorway while simultaneously rocking from side to side; it is all you can do to keep your balance. When you are half-way across the moat and poised perilously above the bright blue smoking liquid, the slab stops moving towards the doorway but continues to sway from side to side. A voice comes from the black marble face: 'You are no Ophidian,' it says, 'and you are certainly not a Black Shadow. No others are permitted to cross, and if you were here on the business of the Archmage Globus you would have known to say the password before stepping on to my tongue. Now, stranger, I have you at my mercy. I should toss you into the moat. But I suppose I could spare you — and I do so love to hear a proud warrior plead for mercy. Plead with me, stranger; beg for your life!' If you want to compose a speech imploring the doorway to spare you, turn to **362**; if you remain stubbornly silent, turn to **31**.

233

The Minstrel stands his harp on the road so that he can fight more easily, but the instrument continues to make music. You can see the strings vibrating and the keening voice seems to emanate from the front of the harp, which is carved in the likeness of a human head. The second boar-faced soldier seems to be dazed by the music and the Minstrel is about to deliver an unopposed death-blow to the first when the third arrives on the scene. He, too, is held in thrall by the haunting melody, but his mount, rearing out of control, treads on the harp and breaks it. The Minstrel kills the first boar-face but the other two recover, dismount, and press home their attack. The Minstrel kills another boar-face before he finally receives a mortal stroke. With his dying effort he despatches the last of the boar-faces, and the road is silent but for an occasional discordant note from the damaged harp. If you want to look more closely at this scene of carnage, turn to **363**; if you would rather use the Aleph, in the hope of travelling to somewhere more welcoming, turn to **91**.

234

You materialize in the air a little way above a meadow and fall awkwardly into the long grass. You feel that you are being watched, and glance up to see the hideous shape of a Spectral Stalker forming in the air. Its eyes search back and forth, and below them the writhing mass of tentacles seems to be sensing your scent on the air. *Test your Trail score.* Roll three dice. If the total is equal to or more than your TRAIL score, turn to **29**; if the total is less than your TRAIL score, turn to **300**.

235

One by one, you take all the items from your backpack and place them on the table. Semeion studies them intently, arranging them into groups and then rearranging them. Not all of them are of interest. He insists that there should be seven significant signs to produce a clear meaning – round objects, he stresses, objects that recall the shape of the Aleph. He is interested in any of the following, if you have them:

A circular inn sign
A plate engraved with a hunting scene
A hollow ball of clay
A toy clown in a glass sphere
A rune-inscribed wheel-hub
A round picture of a conjuror
A map drawn on a wooden ball

If you have all seven items, turn to **132**. If you have them all except for the spherical map, turn to **179**. If you have six of them including the spherical map, turn to **220**. If you have only five items, or less, turn to **360**.

236

Even as you turn towards the Conjuror's assistant you see that she is changing. She is a Were-cat: talons are emerging from the tips of her fur-covered fingers and the pointed ears that seemed to be part of her costume are flicking angrily as she snarls at you. As you lunge and parry in the narrow passage behind the stage, you hear the Conjuror attempting to placate the crowd, which is becoming increasingly impatient and noisy in its calls for the return of the Baron's daughter. Dodging the murderous swipes of the Were-cat's claws, you hear the Conjuror shouting orders to Felice to start the wagon – but she is occupied in fighting you.

WERE-CAT   SKILL 8   STAMINA 10

If you are still alive after four Attack Rounds, you hear the crowd storm on to the stage – turn to **47**.

237

Transfixed as much by pain as by the force of the brilliant beam of light, you barely hear Baratcha's words. 'You are the bearer of the Aleph,' she growls, 'and you must survive to accomplish your destiny.' The Vaskind Queen steps into the deadly beam, shielding you in her massive shadow. Instantly you are free. You stagger aside, turning to see the Vaskind's face contorted in agony as the pressure of the light squeezes the life from her body. 'I am dying, warrior,' she croaks, 'but the sacrifice will be worthwhile if you can defeat the tyrant!' The light flickers and then fades, and Baratcha's lifeless body falls to the floor. You are alone in the silence and gloom of the long hallway. Turn to **386**.

238

Your sword strikes one of the Silica Serpent's eyes, which shatters into a thousand shards. A fountain of black fluid jets from the creature's eye-socket as it dies. As you turn away from the carcass, the Wood Elves who have been watching your fight flee from you in fear. You ignore them and turn your attention to the captive in the net. Turn to 125.

239

The Goblin that you have wounded begins to gibber in terror. His comrade turns, looks up, and screams. The hideous shape of a Spectral Stalker is forming in the air above you. The glittering orbs of its eyes search back and forth, and below them the writhing mass of tentacles seems to be sensing your scent on the air. Add 1 point to your TRAIL score. The Goblins fling themselves through the trapdoor; you hear a splash as they land in the river. The Spectral Stalker becomes more solid with every moment that passes. *Test your Trail score.* Roll three dice. If the total is equal to or more than your TRAIL score, turn to 89. If the total is less than your TRAIL score, turn to 307.

240

You throw yourself from the path of the jet of fluid – but not quickly enough! A spray of liquid splashes across you and as you hit the ground and roll away from the Silica Serpent you feel pain explode all over your body, as if red-hot knives were being pressed into your flesh. The Silica Serpent's venom is a powerful acid: roll one die and deduct the result from your STAMINA. If you are still alive, you pick yourself up, step back — and collide with the leader of a troop of soldiers. They are tall, thin humanoids, totally encased in plate armour made of black glass. Each carries a spear and has a set of pipes hanging from his belt. You are trapped between the soldiers and the Silica Serpent; you have no choice but to surrender. Turn to 306.

241

You can find nothing in your backpack to lighten the gloom, and decide to use the Aleph to leave. You look up to find that the last daylight has died — and the ballerina is staring at you! 'We're coming to play with you,' she says, and starts dancing towards you. Unseen things are moving in the cupboards; the metal soldiers are marching across the floor towards you; the rocking-horse bares its teeth and rocks in your direction; the jester's costume is jerking on its hook; and the door of the room is beginning to creak open!

You are hemmed in by moving toys. You are beginning to feel panic — add 1 point to your TRAIL score. The only way out is through the window. Will you throw open the casement and climb out (turn to 322)? Or would you rather make a stand against this army of toys and ghosts (turn to 350)?

242

You jump and in the same moment the Colepod veers towards you and you are struck by one of its six horny knees. As the creature thunders away into the long grass you hit the ground and tumble head over heels several times before you come to rest. Roll one die and subtract the result from your STAMINA. If you are still alive, you lie in the trampled grass for several minutes recovering your breath. Then, painfully, you stand. Turn to **41**.

243

You walk for hours between towering shelves laden with dusty volumes. No matter how far you go, the corridor extends, without end, as far as the eye can see. At last, however, in a gap between two sets of shelves, you find a door. It is slightly ajar, and the notice on it announces: *Office of the Artefacts Specialist. Please knock and wait.* Below the notice is a heavy brass knocker and below that, set into the wooden beams of the door, are a circular piece of glass and a brass plate with a narrow slit. Will you push the door open and walk through the doorway (turn to **147**), lift the knocker and knock on the door (turn to **198**), or turn away and look for a way out of the Library (turn to **27**)?

244

Roll a die. The result is the number of minutes that you spend in your increasingly frantic search for the door. During all this time dozens of little Shadowlings, hidden in the darkness, are hounding you, leaping on to your body and sucking your blood. You lose STAMINA at the rate of one point each minute. If you survive until you find the door, you pull it open with a sob of relief and slam it shut behind you. You make for your only remaining route – through the door with light showing round its edges. Turn to **324**.

245

The priest howls accusations of trickery and dark magic, but the congregation of Elves is impressed by your escape from certain death. The guards release you and Grondel, and you say farewell to the old Elf. You want to leave the underground city and wander away into the darkness between the decrepit buildings, looking for a secluded place in which to unpack the Aleph. Grondel calls you back, begging you to produce some piece of evidence for his theory that there are worlds beyond the confines of the Elves' cavern. A glimpse of the Aleph, with its teeming display of the infinite worlds of the Macrocosmos, would be enough to convince anyone that other worlds exist. If you agree to show it to Grondel and the priest, turn to **18**; if you hurry into the shadows to use it to travel elsewhere, turn to **377**.

246

The Wood Elves wait, gazing up into the sky; you wait, watching the Wood Elves. Then one of them gives a shout and you see something descending out of the turquoise distance. The Wood Elves scatter, retreating from their netted captive, as an iridescent serpentine form spirals downwards on gossamer wings. It is somewhat like a slim Dragon crossed with a giant winged Centipede. Its scales glitter as it undulates through the air; its head is an armoured mask of silvered glass plates. It floats to the ground and scuttles to the boulder, cutting the ropes that secure the net with fangs like splinters of glass. Its huge eyes, like black pools under glass domes, inspect the contents of the net. Will you continue to watch and wait (turn to **142**), or will you attack the creature while the Elves are absent (turn to **287**)?

247

After walking along the passage for some time you eventually reach a small chamber which has doorways in three of its walls. On the fourth wall, opposite the doorway engraved with the circle and triangle symbol, a plaque has been set into the stone, and on the plaque are inscribed the words *The End*. There seems to be nothing else remarkable about this room, however, and turning to face the doorway with the symbol you choose through which portal you will leave: the one in front of you (turn to **329**), the one to your right (turn to **224**), or the one to your left (turn to **78**).

248

You find yourself standing on a smooth platform that glows but gives out no heat. You are in a chamber lined with walls of opaque glass and polished metal. Rows of coloured lights wink at you and a barely-audible hum and a slight vibration pervade the room. You step off the platform and its glow fades. Suddenly a voice speaks out of the air: *'Unauthorized use of transporter — investigate!'* A second voice asks: *'Is it another specimen?' 'Insufficient data,'* replies the first voice. *'Sending the Grappler.'* You step backwards and bump into a table whose surface is covered with flashing lights and coloured switches. You wonder what would happen if you were to flick some of the switches at random and then jump back on to the platform; if you want to do this, turn to **151**. Alternatively, you could search for a place to hide — turn to **352**. If you would rather just wait for something to happen, turn to **96**.

249

You do exactly as Necromon asks. You drink the sweet liquid and hold the empty flask to your lips, until you are suddenly overwhelmed by a feeling of faintness. Deduct 2 points from your STAMINA. If you are still alive, the last thing you remember is Necromon hurriedly corking the flask while suggesting that you lie down and rest. Then the potion goes to work on your mind. Your thoughts dissolve into patterns of coloured lights mingled with visions of ineffable beauty and significance. Throughout this wonderful display, a small voice in the back of your mind, like a child shouting to be heard in the midst of a Neuburg harvest-time carnival, is trying to tell you to come to your senses. Roll four dice. If the total is less than, or equal to, your STAMINA, turn to **73**; if the total is greater than your STAMINA, turn to **284**.

250

Boosted by the power drawn from you and Semeion by the Energy Leeches, the Telopticon's screen clears once more, and you find yourself looking at the inside of Globus's Citadel. You can see a long, shadowy hall and, at the end of it, a many-faceted dome that glitters like an enormous gem. *This must be Globus's audience chamber*, says Semeion's voice inside your mind, *and that shimmering structure is a Prism of Power, an artefact of high magic. Only its creator, Globus himself, can pass through it. No other living thing can penetrate those glowing facets — although non-living beings, such as the Spectral Stalkers, can pass through unhindered. I fear that even such a Prism would be inadequate to shield you from your relentless pursuers. I sense you are thinking of weapons — of swordblades and arrows; and while it is true that such inanimate objects can pass through the Prism, they can do so only if moving very slowly — so banish any thoughts of trying to throw a spear or a dagger at Globus while he sits within his Prism of Power. The Aleph? Why, yes — the Aleph is beyond most physical and magical laws, and it would pass through the Prism as if it did not exist.* The Energy Leeches can supply no more power: the picture dissolves into swirling colours. Turn to **380**.

The robed being interrupts your greeting. 'You are confused, Lord,' he says. 'That is not surprising. We, the few remaining Feliti — the last of your people — have waited long ages for your return. Now we will prepare the Jewel of Sleep with which you will defeat our evil ruler.' The Feliti busy themselves plucking the purple blooms from the garden plants, while their leader, in a mystical trance, begins another incantation, his hands outstretched over the growing heap of blooms brought to his feet by his people. You are sure that he is reciting a magical formula, but you are not so sure you want to find out what it does. If you decide to take out the Aleph and use its power to travel elsewhere in the Macrocosmos, turn to **365**; if you would rather wait until the spell is cast, turn to **52**.

252

Clouds of Black Shadows are descending on the plains, so you make off in the opposite direction, towards the foot of the vast cliff. As you scramble on to higher ground you look back to see the grasslands littered with dark flapping shapes. As you watch, groups of them start to fly upwards carrying the lifeless bodies of Colepods. You reach a place where a path begins its zig-zag ascent of the cliff-face and, as you have no desire to return to the plains, you decide to climb upwards. Turn to 12.

253

'Don't be alarmed by my appearance,' says the strange wheeled being as you step from the machine into his study. 'I realize that you barbarians don't comprehend the advances of science, but I am quite harmless. I am Metron, the Mapmaker.' You gaze in wonderment at the maps and charts that cover the walls and desks, and, perhaps because they remind you of the Aleph, you are particularly intrigued by a collection of maps that are painted on the surfaces of wooden balls. 'I see you are surprised to see spherical maps,' Metron squeaks. 'No doubt you think the world is flat – or built on terraces, as the fabled Ziggurat World is supposed to be. I can tell you, my friend, that I have studied worlds through-out the Macrocosmos; and whatever shape they are supposed to be, after I have measured and mapped them they are round. But tell me: have you brought anything with you? I am always looking for new objects to measure.'

You wonder which of your items you should ask Metron to examine. If you possess them, you could offer him Cerod the Harp (turn to **346**), a clay ball that rattles (turn to **49**) or a god's Hunting Horn (turn to **173**). If you refuse to allow Metron to see any of your possessions, turn to **375**.

254

Rock-climbing tests both strength and endurance and this wall of rock is as high as the mightiest of the Cloudhigh Mountains of Khul. There are few ledges on which to rest, no gullies or chimneys to provide a change from the relentless necessity of clinging to the bare stone, often carrying all your weight on one tenuous finger-hold, while you search for the next outcrop of rock which will support you. Roll seven dice. If the total is equal to, or less than, the sum of your SKILL and STAMINA, turn to **321**; if the total is greater than the sum of your SKILL and STAMINA, turn to **102**.

255

The Spectral Stalker has failed to find you. You heave a sigh of relief as the hideous creature shakes its great head in frustration and begins to dissolve into the air. The Golem is completely still now; it will be nothing more than a clay statue until the next rainstorm. Now you can make your way to the cave in the cliff-face. Turn to **263**.

256

After several bone-jolting minutes, the Colepod begins to slow its heedless charge. It tosses its head wildly in an attempt to dislodge you; but you hang on grimly, and eventually, defeated, the Colepod comes to a halt. You release your hold only cautiously, but the creature has apparently forgotten its panic already and has resumed the occupation with which it fills nearly all of its waking existence: munching grass. You lean against its flank and recover your breath. Turn to **33**.

After walking for some time you see daylight ahead, and step through a doorway to find yourself in a square courtyard with an undulating floor of burnished metal. Bright sunlight streams down the shaft formed by the walls and is reflected off the floor to illuminate the metal statues that stand on the peaks of the uneven floor. Each statue is of a heroic warrior holding a weapon and a brilliantly polished shield. There are doorways leading from the courtyard, one in each of the four walls; as usual, one of the doorways bears the circle and triangle symbol. As you decide which door- way to take, you notice that the statues are slowly, mechanically, pivoting towards you, metal arms moving to adjust the angle of their shields. The sun's rays, concentrated in the hollows of the metal floor, are being reflected on to the soldiers' shields – and then back at you! As the beams coincide, you are almost struck blind by the dazzling light, and a wall of heat drives you to your knees.

Roll three dice. If the total is equal to or more than your STAMINA, you do not have the strength and will to rise to your feet and run – crushed by the overpowering heat, you slowly roast. Your adventure ends here. If the total is less than your STAMINA, you somehow find the energy to stand and run. Lose 3 points from your STAMINA. Do you run to the doorway you were facing, marked with the symbol (turn to **78**); the one behind you (turn to **122**); the one to your left (turn to **186**); or the one to your right (turn to **285**)?

258

A tunnel slopes upward before you. After following it for some time you reach a junction from which a passage leads downwards and a stairway leads up. Your route lies upwards, you are sure, towards the highest level of this strange tiered world, so you take the stairs. You step on to the first stair, and a shiver passes through your body. You move on to the second step: this time you definitely feel a momentary shudder. You advance gingerly to the third step; but feel nothing. The fourth step, however, gives you a jolt that leaves you cold and trembling. You summon up all your courage to tread on the fifth step; but it does nothing to you, and nor does the sixth. The seventh step catches you unawares with a shock that almost brings you to your knees. However, steps eight, nine, ten and eleven are all harmless, so that by the time you reach the twelfth step you are unprepared for the agonizing spasm that doubles you up in pain. Lose 2 points of STAMINA. It is clear that each jolt is more powerful than the last; the next could be enough to finish you. But how can you tell which steps to avoid? You think you can detect a pattern in the steps that give shocks; and you try to calculate it before continuing the ascent. Which is the next step you should avoid:

The seventeenth step?	Turn to **98**
The nineteenth step?	Turn to **221**
Or the twentieth step?	Turn to **315**

259

You grip the massive tome with both hands and tug it from its shelf. You study the ornate script and realize that the book is an alphabetical list of all types of magicians. The book has fallen open at a page of wizards whose names begin with the letter G – and there, in front of your nose, is the name Globus. You read the following description:

> **GLOBUS**. *Rank*: Archmage.
> *Residence*: The Ziggurat World.
> *Comments*: One of the most powerful images in Macrocosmos, but concentrates on research and experimentation. Specialities include summonings and transportation between the various Spheres of the Macrocosmos. Also theoretical studies of the Aleph, the One Sphere believed to contain all that exists.

You ponder these words. You must assume that the ball you are carrying is the Aleph. Perhaps the flying creature that gave it to you was caught by the Spectral Stalkers while trying to take it to Globus? What will you look for now – a way out of this Library (turn to **27**), or someone who can tell you more about the Aleph (turn to **243**)?

260

You step through a doorway into the dark interior of the rock wall and climb the steep stairs. Turning a corner, you climb towards a window – and looking out of it you find that you are walking sideways: where the sky should be there is instead one of the inner walls of the courtyard! You stagger, seized with vertigo, but force yourself to continue up the stairs; turning another corner, you find that although you are still trudging upwards, when you lift your head you are walking towards the maze-like gardens. You round another corner, and are once again climbing into the dark interior of the rock. You turn another corner, into daylight, to find that the world has righted itself, and you are stepping up to the balcony where Semeion is seated at a stone table. 'The staircases in my house can be confusing at first,' he says with a smile, 'but here you are at last. Please be seated. After your difficult journey to reach me, the least I can do is try to answer any questions you may have.' You sit opposite Semeion. For some reason, you are sure that you can trust the wise old man. Without a word you withdraw the Aleph from your backpack and place it on the stone table. Turn to **65**.

261

Within seconds you are surrounded, and cannot hope to escape. The largest of the Vaskind uses his splay-fingered hands to rend the surface of the huge bubble and pull it over you and his warriors. The bubble descends through clear, green, fish-filled water, before coming to rest against a vast transparent dome resting on a shelf of rock. Within the dome is a settlement of some sort: irregular structures of coral, shell and stone rise from a network of pools and canals. The bubble slides down the surface of the dome, merging into it as you approach the sea bed. The air inside the dome is damp and malodorous, but breathable; you are given little chance to examine your surroundings as the Vaskind hurry you to the centre of the underwater city. You are placed on a low pedestal in the middle of a large, square pool; in front of you rises a throne, empty except for a gold crown. A Vaskind in decorated robes addresses you from the steps of the throne. 'We mean you no harm, stranger,' he croaks, 'but we have not seen your like before. Globus, the Archmage, rules the peoples of this world; are you his friend or his foe?'

If you say that you are Globus's friend, turn to **138**; if you say that you are his enemy, turn to **345**.

262

The ghostly figures pursue you through the castle. You dare not stop to look behind you, but you can feel their chilling presence at your back. You race along dusty corridors, across a small yard, through a doorway, and up a spiral staircase. As you climb, you become aware that your pursuers are no longer behind you, but you continue to climb. At last you reach the top of the stairs and find a door standing ajar. Stepping through it, you find yourself at the top of a tower, in a room illuminated with the dying rays of the setting sun. It is a child's bedroom, crowded with toys. There is only one door, which you close behind you as you enter. The ghostly couple can be neither seen nor heard, and you seem to be safe at last. But nightfall is upon you – will you stay in this room (turn to **38**), or use the Aleph to travel elsewhere (turn to **61**)?

Pulling at the jumble of boulders in the cave entrance, you manage to clear a path into the cave, which is illuminated by large glowing bowls. Mayrek the Potter greets you and thanks you effusively. He looks very tired and thin, and explains that the Golem was one of his experiments that went awry. The creature was intended to be a servant, but it developed a will of its own and imprisoned its creator in the cave which serves as Mayrek's home and workshop. By way of a reward for rescuing him, he tells you that you can take any item from his workshop. You wander among racks of statuary and pottery, each object a fine work of art, but in the end two items attract your attention. One seems very useful: a small porcelain box containing 5 Gold Pieces. The other, a plain ball of glazed clay, intrigues you because its shape and size remind you of the Aleph. Will you choose to take the box (turn to **100**) or the ball (turn to **368**)?

264

In this Attack Round you decide to let fate take its course. *Test your Luck*. If you are Unlucky, your sword slides uselessly along the Silica Serpent's scaly flank — return to **343** and continue your fight with the creature. If you are Lucky, turn to **123**.

265

You rush from the forest and fend off the attack of the second boar-faced soldier. Meanwhile, the Minstrel despatches the dazed soldier who began the attack. The soldier facing you reins back his mount and turns to flee just as a third soldier, riding another gigantic lizard, arrives on the scene and quickly decides that he, too, will retreat. The Minstrel has other ideas, however, and he plucks savagely at the strings of his harp, whose song rises to a painful crescendo. The two boar-faced soldiers cannot resist the music of the harp; with glazed eyes they dismount and trudge back to the Minstrel, who swiftly despatches them. 'A warrior!' he says, turning to you. 'And disguised as I am. A remarkable coincidence. My thanks to you, anyway, stranger.' He points to the bodies of the boar-faced soldiers. 'They are Zwinians. Wretched beings, but they are mine. I am returning to reclaim my birthright from Frampa the Usurper. These scum were clearly loyal to their new master. Will you come with me? Another sword-arm would be useful.' He strums the strings of his harp and produces a sound that seems to call to your very soul. If you do not want to accompany the Minstrel, you can either run away into the forest (turn to **157**) or walk away along the road (turn to **342**); if you agree to go with him, turn to **57**.

266

'If you are a friend of the tyrant Globus,' shrills the Mantir, while his comrades shake their spears angrily, 'you are no friend of the people of the plains. We pay our tribute, which grows more onerous each year. We will offer no more to Globus, or to spies such as you. But you have shown bravery, and you have saved one of our animals so we will let you go in peace. But keep off the plains, stranger!'

Four of the Mantirs guard you closely as you retrace your steps back towards the higher ground at the foot of the cliff. You have nowhere to go but up the path that climbs in a zig-zag up the face of the cliff. Turn to **12**.

267

Wayland listens to your story, then ponders silently for some time. 'I'm an Artefacts expert,' he says at last. 'And, strictly speaking, the Aleph isn't an Artefact. It's not anything, really, on account of it being everything, if you see what I mean. Be that as it may, your real

problem is the Spectral Stalkers. This fellow Globus
may be anxious to take delivery of this here Aleph, but
clever folk have been looking for this item for more
years than there are books in this library, and waiting a
while longer won't hurt anybody. But those Spectral
Stalkers, they don't sound as if they're inclined to wait.
Once you're away from Limbo, use the Aleph to travel.
It will take you where it wants to go. Keep moving and
the Stalkers won't find you. Also, look for Signs and
Portents. Round, the signs will be, like the Aleph itself.
And if you don't understand them, let the Aleph take
you to the sage Semeion Cryptoglyphos: he'll explain
them. But keep moving to avoid danger. And now, you
must leave Limbo.' Wayland points to a doorway
engraved with the word *EXIT*. Dazed by his words,
you step through it. Turn to **185**.

268

You hurl the Aleph at the glowing crystal but objects
can pass through the transparent walls of light only if
they are moving very slowly — and the Aleph merely
bounces off the Prism and falls to the floor. As the
Spectral Stalkers lurch in your direction, you become
frantic with fear, clawing at the transparent Prism with
your bare hands. Tentacles seize your legs and your
last sight is of the Archmage's gloating face.

269

You exchange 2 Gold Pieces for the spherical map of
Titan. Metron also insists that you take several sheets
of paper and a strange writing implement called a
pencil, saying that you never know when you might

need to make a map of your own (record this trans-action on your *Adventure Sheet*). The Mapmaker then busies himself at a desk, making calculations and scrib-bling notes and papers. After a few minutes he turns, and seems surprised to see you. 'Are you still here?' he says. 'Run along now. Can't you see I'm busy? Be off with you!'

If you want to return to the small chamber from which you arrived in the Mapmaker's study, turn to **42**; if you would rather use the Aleph to take you elsewhere, turn to **217**.

270

The Mantir tells you that he wants 8 Gold Pieces in compensation for the Colepod you have killed. If you do not have such a large sum, or are unwilling to pay it, the Mantir says that he will accept a jewel or a finely-worked object of precious metal instead; if you have a Ring of Light, a Jewel of Sleep, a Seven-Pointed Star Talisman, or a Silver Dagger, any one of these items will be acceptable. If you cannot, or will not, offer either the money or one of these items, you will have to fight the duel — turn to **223**.

If you are willing to pay, remember to cross the Gold Pieces or the object from your *Adventure Sheet*. Pleased with this transaction, the Mantirs are making ready to depart, when one of them looks skyward and shrieks in alarm – turn to 388.

271

Restore 1 point of LUCK. You have awoken and acted just in time to save your life. As you leap across the room you realize that the eyes are watching you from a crack in the floorboards – a concealed trapdoor, which begins to open, revealing a Goblin with a knife. But you are already in position to grasp the trapdoor and slam it shut, knocking the Goblin backwards. You stand on the trapdoor and listen in amusement to the confused and angry Goblin voices below. You hear the voices recede, and then the sound of oars paddling through the water as the Goblins return home empty-handed. The Goblin leader dropped his knife inside your room when you slammed the trapdoor on his head. You pick it up; it is a dagger with a carved wooden handle and a blade of pure silver. You may keep it if you want to. As there is no means of securing the trapdoor from inside your room, you stay awake until dawn. Turn to 40.

272

You make slow progress along the dark, rock-strewn valleys. The walls of the ravine are now too high for you to climb, but you feel more secure in the unlit depths. If you have Provisions, you may stop to eat a meal and restore up to 4 points of STAMINA. You stumble on for some time until the steep-sided valley ends at a stone wall. You look up to see that you are at the base of an enormous tower. Stone steps rise from the floor of the canyon and lead to an open stairway that curves upwards round the outside of the tower. You pace cautiously up the stairs until you are on the far side of the tower. You are already far above the ravine, and you feel exposed to view from all sides, but you are still far from the top of the tower. In front of you, set into the massive stonework, is a wooden door that you presume gives access to the interior of the tower. Will you continue up the stairs (turn to **70**); or will you try to open the door (turn to **199**)?

Suddenly the old woman is no longer within the circle of fires, which leap up to form a wall of flames around you. Through the flickering tongues of fire you can see her glaring at you, her hands moving in the air to trace the pattern of a witch's curse. Reduce your LUCK by 1 point. You do not want to risk jumping through the flames; nor do you intend to stay in the cave while the crone casts another spell. You use the Aleph to leave. Turn to **30**.

274

At last the door is free of fungus and the latch is uncovered, but you cannot see it. Drowning in a sea of black, viscous smog, your eyes are blinded by tears of pain and your lungs are filled with poisonous fumes. You scrabble weakly at the wooden door — and, just as you are about to collapse, your hand finds the latch. You pull open the door, fall through it, slam it shut behind you and sink gratefully to the floor of the corridor beyond. The air in these tunnels is not the freshest, but to you it smells as sweet and pure as a mountain breeze. After resting a while, you pick yourself up and continue along the passage. Turn to 148.

275

The Library seems to extend limitlessly in all directions. No matter how far you march along any corridor, it still stretches away ahead of you as far as you can see. The only interruptions in the endless lines of books are the sporadic gaps between the shelves where cross-passages and stairways lead to other corridors. Occasionally the silence is broken by the distant echoes of voices or footsteps, but you meet no one. Sometimes you pause to examine the volumes on the shelves, but only very rarely do you find one that is written in a language you understand. Eventually you plod down a staircase and find yourself at a point where four corridors meet. You have lost all sense of direction, but this crossroads looks very similar to the place where you arrived in the Library, although there is now no *Enquiries* desk. You choose one of the four corridors: turn to either 164, 243, 298 or 373.

276

The grass is taller than you expected and the tallest clumps, towering high above your head, consist of blades as thick and tough as saplings. As you cut a path with your sword, you hear the sound of pounding hooves and crashing vegetation – and suddenly an animal appears, charging straight at you through the grass! It is a Colepod; it resembles a gigantic insect in that it has six legs and a domed carapace, though in size and behaviour it is more like a maddened bull. In a frenzy of fear it bears down on you heedlessly. Will you attempt to thrust your sword into it (turn to 160), seize it with your bare hands and try to grapple it to the ground (turn to 364), or jump out of its path (turn to 75)?

277

You cup your hands and plunge them into the basin; you withdraw them and drink. The liquid *is* water; in fact it is possibly the most refreshing water you have ever tasted, and you realize that it is doing more than merely quenching your thirst. Soon you feel fully fit and ready for anything. Restore your STAMINA to its *Initial* score, and turn to 20.

278

The innkeeper's sword is a doughty weapon, but the innkeeper himself is out of condition. You fight him in the fading light of dusk.

INNKEEPER   SKILL 6   STAMINA 5

If you defeat him, turn to 97.

279

To jump the distance from the middle of the moat to the bank would be difficult under the best of circumstances; to attempt it from a swaying, rocking slab of stone is almost impossible. To make matters worse, just as you exert all the strength in your legs to propel you towards your target, the doorway jerks its 'tongue' towards its 'mouth'. The result is that you suddenly have no base from which to jump and you topple inelegantly into the moat. For a few moments you flail helplessly, before sinking beneath the bright blue ripples for ever.

280

The Grappler is in charge of this survey ship's wildlife collection. It is programmed to tend the various life-forms that are kept in the cages, and to capture any that escape. As far as it is concerned, you are an escaped animal and must be recaptured. Manoeuvering swiftly, it blocks your attempts to sidestep and, extending its telescopic limbs, it closes in on you.

You point *Extinguisher*'s nozzle at the Grappler's head and pull the trigger. Instead of a gout of flame or a blast of explosive pellets, all that emerges from the weapon is a stream of creamy liquid that coats the Grappler's dome but does nothing to slow its attack. Cursing, you dodge its flailing limbs, but as you do so you realize that the creature's movements are becoming less co-ordinated. You scramble over to one side of the room and watch as the viscous fluid, seeping into the Grappler's mechanical innards, makes it run out of control. It collides with the metal cupboard, its arms windmill wildly for a few seconds, and then, in a shower of sparks, it stops moving. Restore 1 point of LUCK. Turn to 55.

281

Expecting another shower of digestive juices at any moment, you scrabble in your backpack for the spherical map. Your eyes are now accustomed to the deep gloom, and you are able to take careful aim before you hurl the ball into the Lithogen's throat. Cross the map from your *Adventure Sheet* then roll two dice. If the total is equal to, or less than, your SKILL, turn to 154; if the total is greater than your SKILL, turn to 165.

282

Across the courtyard an old man is leaning from a balcony. He waves to you. 'Greetings!' he calls. 'I am Semeion, known as Cryptoglyphos because I read the meanings of signs and symbols. You have done well to find my innermost courtyard. If you would speak with me, ascend the staircase below this balcony. The way is longer than it looks, for the stairs twist strangely, but I will await you here.' If you accept this invitation, turn to 260. If you decide instead that you have had enough of Semeion's labyrinthine dwelling, you can use the Aleph to take you elsewhere: you take the sphere from your backpack, and lose yourself in its swirling images – turn to 234.

283

Taking the glowing sphere from your backpack, you gaze into its infinite depths. Instantly you are enthralled by the numberless panoramas that swirl within the Aleph, each scene impossibly small and yet perfectly real. The longer you gaze, the more you can see: men and monsters, humble villages and glittering cities, rolling landscapes and shimmering planets. You feel yourself being enveloped by the Aleph and transported within it. Roll one die. If you roll an even number, turn to **180**. If you roll an odd number, turn to **171**.

284

The small voice in the back of your mind cannot make itself heard. You continue to see the drug-induced parade of visions, even while Necromon is tightening the leather straps that secure you to his table. You die without even the small satisfaction that no part of you will be wasted: Necromon needs strong limbs and organs such as yours to augment the powers of the monster he is creating in his other room.

285

It seems you will walk forever in these shadow-filled corridors that turn to right and left with bewildering frequency — until at last you turn yet another corner and see daylight ahead of you. Ducking through the doorway at the end of the passage, you find yourself in a square courtyard. Sunlight filters down the shaft made by the courtyard's walls to illuminate the tree that grows in the centre of the floor. You circle the tree suspiciously, but it seems to harbour no dangerous creatures. You sit on the bench next to it and read the notice nailed to its trunk:

> *Of Semeion's six outer courts*
> *Two have been made for ease:*
> *Beneath these branches gather thoughts;*
> *The fountain's waters please.*
> *At Semeion's gate there is a block.*
> *Recall then fount and tree;*
> *Their pleasant settings will unlock*
> *The secret of the key.*

There is no sign of a fountain in this courtyard; you assume it must be in another. You rest here and, if you have Provisions, you can eat a meal and restore up to 4 points of STAMINA. Then you decide to move on. Facing the doorway engraved with the circle and triangle symbol, you choose through which doorway you will leave: the one in front of you (turn to **153**), the one behind you (turn to **257**), the one to your right (turn to **317**), or the one to your left (turn to **78**).

286

You place your hand on the door and push, but it will not budge. Determined to move it, you put your shoulder against the centre of the door – and as you do so the brass knocker descends on your head! Lose 2 points of STAMINA. As you fall to the ground, clutching your throbbing cranium, you hear the low voice saying: 'You are a human warrior. You possess eight coins of gold. Please insert four coins into the slot and enter.' Will you pay the door its entrance fee of 4

Gold Pieces and then push it again (turn to **147**); or will you abandon this painful door and look for a way out of the Library (turn to **27**)?

Leaping from the cover of the bush, you are able to strike before the creature is aware of you. But although your sword shatters several of its scintillating scales, the creature seems to be unharmed, and twists round to face you. It is a Silica Serpent, a dangerous adversary. Glassy scales protect its head and body, it moves very quickly, snapping at you with its fang-filled mouth and each time it attacks it squirts from its face a jet of acid that corrodes anything it touches.

SILICA SERPENT   SKILL 7   STAMINA 11

Each combat round, after you have resolved the combat between your sword and the Serpent's fangs, compare Attack Strengths a second time. If you win, or the scores are the same, you have avoided the jet of acid; but if you lose, you are splashed with the liquid and must lose 2 points of STAMINA. Keep a note of the number of Attack Rounds you fight. If at any time you decide to use your LUCK in combat, turn to **110**. If you are still alive after four Attack Rounds, turn to **50**.

You put the pipes to your lips and blow softly into them. Strange, discordant notes float into the air and the effect on the Silica Serpent is immediate. The creature cocks its great head on one side, like a dog listening to its master's voice. As you continue to play, it curls its long body into a circle and goes to sleep. Not daring to cease piping, you tiptoe past the scaly monster — and then continue on your way towards the Vitreous Citadel. Turn to **336**.

289

You fling open the door, grab your backpack and jump from the wagon, landing on the pitted surface of the stony road. Roll one die and subtract half the result from your STAMINA (round fractions up). If you are still alive, you crawl painfully into the shade of a hedgerow and inspect the contents of your pack. Amazingly, nothing has been broken — restore 1 point of LUCK — and you find that somehow you have collected one of the Conjuror's small, circular calling-cards. It displays the words *Marvip the Magician* above a picture of a tall figure with a black cloak and a glowing wand. The shape of the card reminds you of the Aleph, so you keep it. As you are alone on the road and can see no travellers or settlements, you decide to use the Aleph to go elsewhere. Turn to **63**.

290

You press the button on the right-hand part of the design. Nothing happens — except that you are sure the floor shudders slightly. If you want to remain here in the hope of trying the other button, turn to **95**; if you decide to return along the tunnel turn to **122**.

291

You are aware of feeling sick and weary. Your limbs ache. You can feel ropes tied tight around your wrists and your torso. You force your eyes to open.

You are tied to a stone pillar at the top of a round tower. The pillar is one of many that rise from the perimeter of the flagstone floor to support the tower's roof, and there are prisoners tied to most of the other pillars. You seem to be the only human; among the others are an Elf woman, an amphibious Vaskind and one of the four-legged, insect-like Mantirs. Perched on the parapet that surrounds this topmost level of the tower are several Black Shadows; two more are crouched at your feet, investigating the contents of your backpack. Your heart sinks as they find the Aleph and begin to chatter excitedly. However, it seems they dare not keep it, for they leave it, with your other belongings, at the foot of your pillar. Then, after ensuring that all the prisoners are securely roped, all the Black Shadows take to the air and flap upwards, speeding urgently towards the top of the cliff that overlooks even this soaring tower-top. Once they are out of sight, you begin to struggle in your bonds; but despite your efforts you cannot escape, nor can you reach your sword or your pack. You look hopelessly at your possessions, scattered at your feet. If, among them, you have a clown puppet in a glass ball, turn to **56**; if not, turn to **205**.

292

You follow the twisting tunnel, aware of side-passages and junctions, and soon you are blundering about in a black labyrinth of subterranean paths. At last you see light: the shape of a door outlined by a yellow gleam. You step through into a small room furnished as a study. Avoiding an area of the floor on which arcane symbols have been chalked, you move towards the log fire that is blazing in the fireplace, only to awaken the red-robed old woman who is dozing in an armchair. She stares at you in horror before stammering that you should not be here in her workroom. You try to assure her that you mean no harm, and she begins to relax. You explain that you are trying to escape from Syzuk the Devastator, and she smiles at you. 'Drink this,' she says, pouring a thick brown liquid from a bottle into a pewter flagon. 'It will restore your strength and calm your nerves.' You sniff the liquid: it smells wholesome, like a good vegetable soup, and you drink it. The old woman – Glund's Chief Priestess – told no lies: the drink restores up to 4 points of STAMINA. It also relaxes you, and within a minute you are completely paralyzed! She summons a squad of Skeletal Warriors, who knock you unconscious and carry you away. Turn to 215.

293

Roll one die. The result is the number of minutes that you spend in your increasingly frantic search for an exit from this benighted cave. During all this time dozens of little Shadowlings, hidden in the darkness, are hounding you, leaping on to your body and sucking your blood.

You lose STAMINA at the rate of one point for each minute you remain in the room. If you survive, your flailing arms discover, not one, but two tunnels leading from the cave. Feeling your way with your hands, you take a few steps along each of them before deciding which one to use. Both tunnels are narrow, but seem passable; will you take the one that leads downward (turn to 196), or the one that leads upward (turn to 258)?

294

You emerge from your hiding place and the Wood Elves turn to stare at you in amazement. If you have the rune-inscribed hub of a war-chariot wheel, you know that Elves fear it; if you decide to produce it from your backpack turn to 313. Otherwise, hoping that they are friendly, you speak to them in greeting – turn to 150.

295

This move saves your own life, but it loses the game for Drawenna. You can attack the black warrior in front of you, but he can defend himself simply by turning his well-armoured back on you. Your two white comrades succeed in killing the black warrior caught between them – but then it is the turn of the black side to make a move and attack. Turn to 228.

296

An Elf Woman is tied to the nearest column. 'I cannot tell who or what you are, stranger,' she says in a weak voice, 'but please release us and help us to escape from

here if you can.' As you cut through her bonds, you ask
her why she and the other captives are kept here. 'The
Black Shadows keep prisoners at the top of each of
their towers,' she replies. 'They suck our blood for
food. This turret is a larder for the Black Shadows – and
they will return soon to feed. Release the others,
quickly!' Soon you have released a motley troop of
captives, all of them anxious to leave the tower. Will
you lead them down the staircase that spirals precariously round the outside of the tower (turn to 14); or
through the trapdoor in the centre of the flagstone
floor (turn to 192)?

297
The doorway is real, but the stairs are an illusion that
conceals a wide crevasse in the rocks – into which you
fall. Your adventure ends here.

298
You have been walking for what feels like hours between the towering shelves of books, when you stop in
amazement: you have found a door at last, set into the
side of one of the bookcases. The door is ajar, and you
can hear the murmur of voices beyond it. A large sign
on the door announces:

CLASSIFICATION DEPARTMENT
NO ADMITTANCE

Will you enter (turn to 11)? Or would you rather return
to the crossroads and try one of the other corridors
(164, 373 or 243)?

299

You are indeed in luck. Something is falling towards you: a rope, unrolling as it drops. You grab it, wind it about your arm and cling to it helplessly. Several Ophidians scuttle down the sheer wall of rock with the agility of insects, and half drag, half carry you upwards. At the entrance to the cave, they use the rope to bind you tightly. Two tunnels lead away into the darkness; you are carried along the left-hand passage and into a cavern full of tethered Silica Serpents, each one guarded by several Ophidians. Turn to 53.

300

The Spectral Stalkers have found you! As the first monstrosity turns towards you, and you see yourself reflected a thousand times in the facets of its huge eyes, two others are rapidly taking shape. You try to flee but with an insect-like bound one of them jumps in front of you. You are surrounded. In desperation you strike out, but your blows have no effect on these unnatural creatures. Their talons rake your body; their tentacles rope about your limbs. Screaming in fear, you lose consciousness. Your final thought is that both your quest and your life are over.

If you have a clay ball that rattles, turn to 325; if not, turn to 54.

301

Soon you are standing alongside the Elf Grondel, your ankles shackled. 'I'm sorry,' the old Elf says, 'I didn't mean to involve you in this dispute. Now we are both doomed.' You point out that as he was able to summon you to this underground city, surely he has the power to free himself. 'My powers were exhausted in bringing you here,' he sighs, casting a worried glance up to the huge mouth-spout that looms over you, 'and now Vacavon will rain death upon us. The water that flows from yonder spout is poisoned: when it falls upon us, it will instantly rot our flesh. Nothing can save us from the downpour.'

If you have a bottle of Siccator, and want to share it with Grondel, turn to **71**; if you have an Umbrella, turn to **144**; if you want to abandon Grondel to his fate, and use the Aleph to escape, turn to **377**; but if you decide to do nothing but wait patiently in your chains, turn to **166**.

302

You start to shiver as soon as you cross the threshold. The room is as cold as a winter night – and the huge cube is a solid block of ice. You peer into the centre of the block: embedded at the heart of the ice is a dark, humanoid shape. You notice an ironic sign: *Here is preserved an enemy of Globus – behold her Power and Majesty!* You notice that the surface of the ice-block is running with water and when you touch the block, shards of ice fall away. The entire cube is only just frozen, and would melt easily if you could provide a source of heat. If you have a Glowcandle or a Heat-sword, and want to try to melt the ice, turn to **376**; otherwise, you leave this room and, crossing the ante-chamber, you step through the dark doorway – turn to **118**.

303

Your white comrade on square *E6* accepts your decision and moves forward to *D6*. He turns to face you. The black warrior on square *E5* suddenly realizes that he is between you and your white comrade, and he turns back and forth in a futile attempt to use his armour to shield himself from attack from two opposite sides. As if it has a life of its own, your pike descends to a horizontal position and lunges repeatedly at the black warrior; your comrade's weapon does the same. In an instant the black warrior is dead. There are no more attacks that can successfully be made by the white side; now it is the turn of the black side to make a move and attack. *Test your Luck*. If you are Lucky, turn to **228**; if you are Unlucky, turn to **32**.

304

'We are subjects of Globus,' shrills the Mantir leader, 'but we hate him. He demands tributes which are more onerous with each passing year; his foul pets terrorize our herds and the peoples of our tribes. We can do nothing against him – for we cannot hope to scale the cliffs to reach him. All I can do is to offer you some information which might help you. At the top of yonder cliffs is the second tier of this world. Avoid the towers of the Black Shadows, and go instead towards the caves of the Ophidians, the keepers of the Silica Serpents. They will not welcome you – they, too, are Globus's creatures – but they are less dangerous than the Black Shadows. Steal, if you can, a set of Ophidian pipes: the music of this instrument controls Silica Serpents. Beyond, on the third tier, is the Crystal Garden, as deadly as it is beautiful, and guarded by more Silica Serpents: and in the midst of the Garden is the Vitreous Citadel, where Globus sits and plots. That place must be your goal.'

As he finishes his speech, one of the Mantirs looks skyward and gives a shriek of alarm. Turn to **388**.

305

You walk towards the daylight and, ducking under a lintel engraved with the circle and triangle motif, you find yourself back at the entrance to the maze. You wander across the rocky ledge, but can find no path either up or down the face of the cliff. It is then that you notice that the large flat-topped boulder near the portal has something etched into its surface – a map of the maze. (The diagram and the words that accompany it are reproduced on the inside front cover of this book. You may study this and, if you accepted pencil and paper from Metron the Mapmaker, you may make a copy of it — in other words you may refer to the diagram at any time during your travels in the maze.) Also on the boulder is a package: you open it and find a meal which, if you eat it, can restore up to 4 points of STAMINA. Written on the package is the message: *Semeion's abode is not easy to discover; try again, traveller, if you seek enlightenment.*

The sun is high in the sky, and you feel in need of a rest in the warmth. You doze and fall into a deep sleep which lasts through the night. You wake at dawn to see the sun rising above the highest of the distant mountains. If you decide to make another attempt to enter Semeion's maze, turn to **149**; if you prefer to use the Aleph to travel elsewhere, you pull the glowing sphere from your pack and stare into it, allowing yourself to be enveloped by the teeming images — turn to **234**.

306

The soldiers are Ophidians, a people who, as you are about to witness, have the skills to control the Silica Serpents. Two of the Ophidians guard you; the others surround the Serpent which, although trapped, is anything but harmless: it spits jets of corrosive liquid at the Ophidians. The acid has no effect on the Ophidians, however, as it merely runs off their glassy plates of armour, and they pay almost no attention to the creature's angry splutters. Instead, one takes the pipes from his belt and begins to play upon them; there is no recognizable tune but the Silica Serpent seems to find the music very relaxing. It stops spitting and struggling, and the Ophidians move in to muzzle its scaly jaws and bind up its diaphanous wings. At this point one of your guards goes to assist his comrades, leaving only one Ophidian watching over you. It seems that now is the best moment for you to escape. If you want to make a break for it you must first vanquish the one remaining guard – turn to **327**; if you would rather remain a prisoner of the Ophidians, turn to **133**.

307

The Spectral Stalkers have found you! As the first monstrosity turns towards you, and you see yourself reflected a thousand times in the facets of its huge eyes, two others are rapidly taking shape. You try to flee but with an insect-like bound one of them jumps in front of you. You are surrounded. In desperation you strike out, but your blows have no effect on these unnatural creatures. Their talons rake your body; their tentacles rope about your limbs. Screaming in fear, you lose consciousness. Your final thought is that both your quest and your life are over.

Roll three dice and deduct the total from your STAM-INA. If, by some miracle, you are still alive, you regain your senses, groaning, your body racked with pain. You have survived the onslaught of the Spectral Stalkers; but where have they taken you? Turn to **392**.

308

Semeion escorts you up another of his curious staircases and into a long room lined with shelves. He tells you the room is his library, but you can see no books. The shelves are full of smooth metal cylinders, one of which Semeion takes and places at the centre of a disc which is set into the top of a tall thin cabinet. The disc is a turntable that Semeions operates with his foot; and as the cylinder rotates with the disc, Semeion brushes it lightly with his fingers. He stops the disc and turns to you. 'I know only a little about Globus,' he says. 'He is an Archmage, a senior magician of great power. His home is the Ziggurat World; he lives on the topmost tier, in a well-guarded Citadel. Surrounding the Citadel is the Crystal Garden, of which I know only that it is beautiful but deadly. There is a secret passage that runs to the Citadel from the level below the Crystal Garden. One more thing: by a lucky chance, the Ziggurat World is one of the realms that is ethereally connected to the Telopticon – a device which enables me to see afar without leaving here. Would you like to try to see Globus's home world? Or perhaps we could spy on the Spectral Stalkers?'

Do you want to attempt to use the Telopticon (turn to 332)? Or are you becoming impatient with Semeion's vague words, and anxious to leave (turn to 23)?

309

You put the Horn to your lips and blow. The first blaring note is enough to terrify the creatures that were about to attack you, scattering them like leaves in a gust of wind; then, although you have exhausted the breath in your lungs, the noise from the Horn continues, becoming ever louder. Swarms of Black Shadows rise into the air in frantic confusion and soon the whole mass of them is disappearing skywards. At last the Horn's blast fades. The Mantirs pick themselves up from the ground and, once they have regained their senses, they overwhelm you with thanks. They depart to gather the scattered herds of Colepods, but the leader asks you to remain here, promising to return with a reward for your help. A little later he canters back to you, bearing a gift of honeycake (which you can eat; it restores up to 4 points of STAMINA) and a weapon in a brightly-decorated scabbard. He explains that the weapon is a Heatsword; when unsheathed, the blade becomes hot without losing the keenness of its edge. When you strike an opponent, it will cause the loss of 1 additional point of STAMINA. After thanking the Mantir, you make your way back to the place where a path begins its ascent of the vast cliff. Turn to **12**.

310

You step through the curtain and into a dark, narrow

passage that runs along the length of the wagon. You overhear the Conjuror, on the other side of the curtain, whispering instructions to his assistant. 'Felice!' he hisses. 'Put the warrior in the back room with the girl, then get to the front. I'll keep this bunch of peasants guessing with some spiel or other. Then, when I shout, lash the horses and we'll make a break for it.' The cat-woman purrs in agreement, and brushes aside the curtain to join you in the passage. She points to a door at one end, and pushes you towards it. If you decide to let yourself be shoved into the back room, turn to **24**. If you stand your ground and defend yourself against the cat-woman, turn to **236**. If you want to try to escape by running through the curtain, across the stage and into the crowd, turn to **361**.

311

To jump the distance from the middle of the moat to the bank would be difficult under the best of circumstances: to attempt it from a swaying, rocking slab of stone is almost impossible. However, just as you are exerting all the strength in your legs to propel you towards the doorway, the doorway itself helps you by jerking its 'tongue' into its 'mouth'. Although this sudden movement was intended to finish you off, it provides extra momentum for your jump and you land on the end of the stone slab just as it is disappearing into the doorway. You stumble, fall and almost slip into the moat; then you recover, scrabble for the slab and somehow manage to hold on. You have succeeded in entering the Vitreous Citadel. Turn to **189**.

312

Gratefully, you drain the flagon of ale. Shortly afterwards you fall into a drugged stupor and fail to wake up even when the Goblins enter your room through the secret trapdoor. The local gossip about the inn is correct: the innkeeper sells his guests to the man-eating Goblins. Your adventure ends here.

313

You pull the wheel-hub from your backpack and reveal its runic inscription to the Wood Elves. One glance at it is enough to send them running into the woods, wailing in terror. You turn your attention to the captive in the net. Turn to 125.

314

'I am the Oracle,' the old woman cackles, 'and you are a warrior on a perilous quest. I sense that you carry a great burden and are hunted by fell and remorseless creatures. But all this you know, and all too well, I suspect. Tell me something that you do not yet understand and I will unravel it for you.'

You are almost speechless with shock after the events in the sunlit parkland and your sudden arrival in this cave, but you manage to stammer an account of your recent experiences. You show the crone the Hunting-Horn. 'I can explain these things,' she says. 'But first, give me gold! Two pieces of gold to hear the words of the Oracle!' This demand takes you by surprise. If you give her 2 Gold Pieces, deduct them from your *Adventure Sheet* and turn to 111; if you are unwilling or unable to pay, turn to 273.

315

Holding your breath at every step, you climb upwards. You reach the nineteenth step without feeling the slightest tremor. Carefully, you leap over the twentieth without touching it, and land on the twenty-first step. Nothing happens and you advance confidently up the rest of the stairway. You have no way of knowing how many more steps are booby-trapped, of course, so to be safe you avoid the thirty-third, the fifty-fourth, the eighty-eighth, and so on. There are many hundreds of stairs, and your brain reels with the mental arithmetic required to work out the next step you have to miss. Eventually, though, you reach the top and push through a trapdoor to find yourself in a cellar. Dim light filters through metal grilles in the ceiling. An open staircase climbs up one of the walls and leads to a door that, you presume, gives on to an upper storey. The walls of the cellar are lined with storage jars, each one almost as tall as you. Will you climb the stairs and go through the door (turn to 189), or investigate the contents of the jars (turn to 355)?

316

You place the bundle on your knees and unfold the cloth to reveal a glowing sphere not much larger than your fist. At first you think it is made of glass, and transparent; but you peer into it and realize that it is made of nothing — or, rather, of many things, countless things. You see oceans, deserts and cities; suns, moons and stars; animals and people; and many things that you cannot recognize. You look and look, and the sphere seems to expand until it is surrounding you.

Then it shrinks to its former size — and you are no longer in the countryside near Neuburg.

You are in a vast building. On all sides, corridors stretch away as far as your eyes can see. Every wall is lined from floor to ceiling with shelves, and every shelf is full of books. In front of you is a desk, over which hang two signs. One says *SILENCE!*, and is completely unnecessary as there is not a sound to be heard. The other says *ENQUIRIES*. There is a little brass bell on the desk. You cover the strange sphere again and put it in your backpack. Will you now set off to search this strange building (turn to **275**) or ring the bell (turn to **6**)?

317

Your walk along the winding passage is uneventful until you reach a junction between tunnels. You are in a tiny square chamber, its vaulted ceiling supported by pillars set in its four corners. Three of the walls consist of open doorways; the other is of finished stone, and bears an inscription: *So near to Semeion, and yet so far to travel.* You face the one doorway that has the circle and triangle symbol above it, and choose which doorway you will leave through:

The doorway before you	Turn to **101**
The doorway behind you	Turn to **285**
The left doorway	Turn to **153**

318

At last you reach the top of the stairway where a gap in the parapet allows you to enter the flagstone-floored turret that is the tower's top storey. Stone pillars rise from the perimeter of the floor to support the tower's roof; there are prisoners tied to most of the pillars. None of the prisoners is human; you can see an Elf woman, an amphibious Vaskind and one of the four-legged, insect-like Mantirs. As you step cautiously across the floor the prisoners raise their heads to stare at you in amazement. Turn to **296**.

319

The big man is jovial, but retains his grip on his sword. 'Welcome, stranger!' he booms, 'to the Inn of the Ghostly Visitors. Don't be alarmed by the name of my fine establishment – it's just my little joke! You know this part of the world? Then you'll have heard the stories. Folk say this place is haunted – that people disappear mysteriously in the night. A load of old wives' tales. Don't believe a word of it. Anyway, this is the only inn for leagues around, so you don't have much choice. You can take the ferry across the river in the morning. Now get inside, and go upstairs — I've a room ready for you.' He points his sword at you threateningly. It is true that you need somewhere to stay for the night, but the innkeeper's attitude makes you suspicious and angry. If you decide to fight him after all, turn to **278**; if you accept his offer of accommodation, turn to **222**.

320

'So you think I'll attack you, do you?' snarls the Logic Dog. 'Well, you're quite right; and therefore, because you have guessed correctly, I should let you pass. But if I let you pass, your guess will be wrong; and if your guess is wrong, as I have already promised, I will attack you. Therefore I have no choice but to attack!' With that, the huge beast prepares to launch itself at you. If you think there is a flaw in the Logic Dog's reasoning, and want to argue with it, turn to **197**; otherwise, prepare to defend yourself — turn to **163**.

321

At last you reach the top of the cliff and stand upon the topmost tier of the Ziggurat World. You clamber over a stone parapet, drop down the other side – and are greeted by a sight that could scarcely be a greater contrast with the bleak aridity of the rocky wasteland below. In front of you stretches the Crystal Garden, a vista of vivid colours and unnatural beauty. Jade flag-stones surround azure fountains, full not of water but of tinkling crystal shards; marble trees stand stiffly above vibrant flowers of coloured glass. Through the lifeless, scintillating vegetation you can see the shimmering domes and towers of the Vitreous Citadel, home of the Archmage Globus. Paths paved with opalescent frag-ments criss-cross the Garden – but each is guarded by a Silica Serpent, tethered to the spot but otherwise free to attack any passer-by. To reach the Citadel you will have to confront at least one Silica Serpent (turn to 162) – unless you leave the paths and try to force a way through the beds of glass flowers (turn to 77).

322

You have clambered through the window and started to climb downwards before you think to look where you are. You are hanging by one hand from the sill of the highest window in the castle, at the top of one of the towers, overhanging the gorge which appears as a black gulf below you. You start to pull yourself back upward, but the rocking-horse bites your hand. You cry out, let go of the windowsill – and your fading scream is cut off by a distant thud as your body lands in the gorge. The haunted Nursery Tower has claimed another victim.

323

The crowd of green-skinned people draws back as you run across the garden and out of the gates. 'Stop!' shouts the robed leader, but you have gone. 'We must stop him! After him, Feliti brothers and sisters! Bring back our Champion!' There is a village outside the garden; the dwellings are old and dilapidated, but you assume they are inhabited and you turn away, racing across a desolate landscape of craggy hillocks and shrubby thickets. You turn to look at your pursuers, and see the Feliti people running from the walled garden – and as they emerge they change! Each one drops to all fours and with a wailing cry is transformed into a long, low hunting beast – like a Giant Weasel, with green fur and a snout full of sharp teeth. You run on, into endless grassy plains in which your pursuers are perfectly camouflaged. The gigantic sun is setting; you run until you are exhausted, and as you stop you are immediately surrounded by a circle of Feliti creatures. You can run no further: you must fight (turn to 68), or surrender to the Feliti (turn to 219).

324

You push open the door and step into a room illuminated by torches. The first thing that strikes you is the rank odour that fills the room; you begin to understand its origin when you see the bloodstained butcher's table standing in the centre of the room, and the large jars containing limbs and internal organs preserved in fluids of various colours. Anatomical diagrams of several sorts of creatures are nailed to the walls. As you close the door behind you, another opens in the opposite wall and a small man in a bloodstained white coat enters, and stops in surprise on seeing you. 'A warrior!' he exclaims. 'A live being! This is most unusual. The only people I ever see are the few lifeless husks that I can beg from those beastly Black Shadows – for my research, you understand. I am Necromon, by the way; perhaps you've heard of me? No? Well, I'm not surprised. I've been down here for many years. I used to be apprenticed to the Archmage Globus, you see, but we had a falling out. Now I live wretchedly here in this macabre dungeon, spending all my time building the tool with which I intend to take my revenge on Globus. Will you assist me, warrior?'

If you agree to hear Necromon's proposal, turn to **108**; if you decline, and say you want to continue on your way, turn to **383**.

325

You regain consciousness to find yourself lying on a marble floor. You know that you should be dead but by some miracle you are alive, and unharmed. Your next thought is for the Aleph, and you rummage frantically in your backpack; the glowing sphere is there, and undamaged, but the clay ball has crumbled into dust. You marvel at your good fortune and at the life-preserving skill of Mayrek the Potter. But perhaps your luck is not so good: you have survived the onslaught of the Spectral Stalkers, but where have they brought you? Turn to **392**.

326

You have only two possible moves. Will you move to the square on your left (square *F3*)? If so, turn to **295**. Or will you move forward (to square *E4*)? Turn to **10**.

327

You throw yourself at the Ophidian guard. He has only a split second in which to block your attack with his spear. He throws a glance towards his comrades, clustered round the trapped Silica Serpent, but you are upon him again. The two of you fall to the ground together, locked in close combat.

OPHIDIAN   SKILL 7   STAMINA 7

Add 1 point to your TRAIL score. After three Attack Rounds of combat, if you are still alive, the other Ophidians are beginning to realize that your opponent needs their assistance. If you have by now killed the Ophidian guard, turn to **35**; if he is still alive, turn to **359**.

328

The Ranganathans have eight fingers on each hand, and each fingernail is as sharp as a razor. They advance, squealing excitedly. You retreat into a corner so you can fight them one at a time.

	SKILL	STAMINA
First RANGANATHAN	5	6
Second RANGANATHAN	5	5
Third RANGANATHAN	7	7

If you defeat them all, you spend some time searching their room. All of the books you find are unintelligible, but in a drawer of the desk you find a jar of clear liquid bearing the label *Corrective Fluid*, which you may take with you. You then return to the crossroads and begin another long hike down one of the other corridors; turn to either 164, 243 or 373.

329

The tunnel ends at a doorway. You step through and find yourself in a small rectangular room with a doorway set in each of the walls. Hanging in the shadows close to the ceiling is a large bundle, which you ignore until you hear a piteous moan and see that the bundle has started to move feebly. Will you investigate (turn to 200), or concentrate on choosing your exit (turn to 45)?

330

The invisible force presses into you like bands of steel closing about you. The pain is becoming unbearable;

consciousness is slipping away. Roll six dice. If the total is less than your STAMINA, turn to **212**; if the total is equal to, or greater than, your STAMINA, turn to **372**.

331

The runic inscription on the wheel-hub strikes terror into the hearts of the Elves and they scatter in all directions. You turn towards the captive, Grondel, and he almost faints from fear until you remember to put away the terrifying object. The courtyard is empty now, and you have time to unshackle the old Elf, who thanks you profusely. You want to leave the underground city and wander away into the darkness between the decrepit buildings, looking for a secluded place in which to unpack the Aleph. Grondel calls you back, begging you to produce some piece of evidence for his theory that there are worlds beyond the confines of the Elves' cavern. A glimpse of the Aleph, with its teeming display of the infinite worlds of the Macrocosmos, would be enough to convince anyone that other worlds exist. If you agree to show it to Grondel and the priest, turn to **18**; if you hurry into the shadows to use it to travel elsewhere, turn to **377**.

332

Semeion takes you to a chamber, deep within his strange home, which houses his Telopticon. The strange device consists of a hoop of metal within which bright colours ceaselessly swirl; connected to the hoop with bundles of wires like knotted vines are two helmets. Semeion dons a helmet; you do likewise, and immediately see that the colours in the hoop are clearing, to be replaced by a picture of a world hanging in space. The picture moves closer; the world is the Ziggurat World, flat tiers of land enclosed within a sphere that is half dark, half light. Closer: you see Globus's Citadel, its shining domes and spires rising from the sparkling brilliance of the Crystal Garden – and then the scene dissolves into swirling colours once more. You hear Semeion's voice inside your mind: *Globus has protected his Citadel with enchantments. I can try to penetrate his defences, but the effort will absorb certain essential salts from our bodies. I know I can withstand the drain of strength – but can you, warrior?*

If you are determined to see inside Globus's Citadel, whatever the cost, turn to **99**. If you would rather try to use the Telopticon to see the Spectral Stalkers, turn to **380**. If you are anxious to continue your travels, turn to **23**.

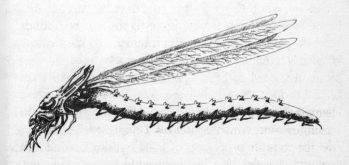

333

You lead the little army of ex-captives through the maze of rocky ravines, heading for the point at which you emerged on this level from the cliff-face path. Eventually your group arrives at the edge of the cliff and you begin the long descent that will take the Elves, Vaskind and Mantirs to their homes — taking with them, perhaps, the seeds of a new spirit of co-operation between the various peoples of the Ziggurat World. A little way down the cliff, however, you bid farewell to the motley group; they no longer need your guidance and you have arrived at the point where the cliff-face path forks. Although you are tempted to return to the hero's welcome that will greet you if you return home with the prisoners you have rescued, you know that you must explore more of this strange world. You set off up the left-hand path; turn to **146**.

334

In the dark the garden is an eerie place. The statues seem to be watching you; the fragrance of the flowers is overwhelming. You decide to leave, but at that moment the robed Feliti appears at the gate. 'We were once a proud and populous people,' he says as he walks into the garden, 'with many fine cities and palaces and parks. Now all is waste, and only this garden survives. But the centuries of watching and waiting were not wasted — because you have arrived to save us. Go now, in darkness: my poor accursed people hunt in their animal forms only in daylight, so you will be safe from them until dawn. Go to the Tyrant's castle, find him and kill him, and release the Feliti from his curse.'

Will you go to the Tyrant's castle (turn to **379**), or use the Aleph to leave this world (turn to **365**)?

335

This tunnel is very dark. You creep forwards, using your hands more than your eyes, and at last you reach – a dead end! There is a wall of rock in front of you. Then you hear a noise, an ominous sound of grinding rocks, and you feel the floor move slightly under your feet. If there is a way forward, the door must be concealed; but perhaps this cul-de-sac is simply a booby-trap for unwary explorers. If you want to remain here to search the walls, turn to **168**; if you would rather return along the tunnel, turn to **122**.

336

Having reached the centre of the Crystal Garden, you stand gazing up at the shimmering windowless walls of the Vitreous Citadel. It is a collection of marvellous structures, each vying with the others to amaze the mind and dazzle the eye: towers of amber and jet, canopies of faceted crystal, domes like enormous pearls, walls that seem to be cataracts frozen while in motion — all reflected in each other's glazed surfaces. The entire edifice is surrounded by a wide moat filled with a bright blue liquid; spirals of smoke rise ominously from its surface. You walk around the Citadel and find that there is only one bridge across the moat: a slab of stone, with one end resting on the bank at your feet, extends across the moat and disappears into the only doorway through the Citadel's curtain wall. The doorway is surrounded by a frame of black marble, carved into an abstract representation of a face, the doorway itself being the mouth, and the stone bridge being the tongue. To reach the Citadel you must either cross the bridge (turn to **232**), or try to wade across the moat (turn to **378**).

337

Dodging the first boulder-breaking blow of the Golem's mallet, you sprinkle the Siccator in a wide arc. (Cross the Siccator from your *Adventure Sheet*.) The drops of liquid sparkle in the air and splash across the Golem's clay torso. The effect is instantaneous: the Golem halts in mid-stride as the slick surface of water evaporates from its body. Cracks appear as the monster attempts to move, and as the Siccator extracts every drop of moisture from the clay the Golem's extremities begin to crumble. After one final shudder, the Golem is motionless, nothing more than a clay statue, rapidly crumbling into a large heap of fine brown dust. You turn away and head for the cave in the cliff. Turn to **263**.

338

You advance towards the Prism of Power, shielding your eyes from the incandescent tracery that pulses across its facets. You press the Aleph against one of the surfaces. After some resistance, the sphere slowly enters the Prism and drops into the waiting hands of the Archmage. For several seconds he gazes at it in wonderment; then a ferocious scowl disfigures his noble countenance.

'At last I have it!' he says. 'At last the Aleph is in my hands. You foolish mortal! You have slaved and suffered to bring me the one tool I need to become Lord of all the Macrocosmos. Every being will bow down before me.' Nothing can save you. You have failed in your quest.

339

As you reach up to grasp the huge cocoon, it drops towards you, splitting open along its underside to reveal a moist, fetid interior ringed with fang-like spines. There is nobody inside. You are being attacked by a Karanth, a cunning creature that has the ability to use some of the intelligence of the prey that it consumes.

The Karanth falls on top of you, attempting to enfold and smother you. Before you can reach a weapon, you find yourself gripped within the Karanth's spines, your skin already being corroded by its digestive juices. You will die unless you can survive without breathing until the Karanth loosens its grip.

Roll four dice; if the total is equal to or more than your STAMINA, you gasp for air but breathe in only the Karanth's mucus secretions — your adventure ends here. If however, the total is less than your STAMINA, you are still conscious when the Karanth, assuming you to be dead, briefly relaxes. Pushing with all your might, you burst from the Karanth's hold and stagger away from the creature. Breathing heavily, you take stock of yourself, and are pleased to find that you have no substantial wounds. The Karanth closes its body and hoists itself up to the ceiling; you have to decide through which doorway to leave — turn to **45**.

340

You draw your sword and advance towards the Dragon. She growls and flames flicker from her snout. 'Typical!' she splutters. 'You young hooligan; no respect for erudition and literature. Weapons are not permitted in the Library in Limbo, so I'm just going to have to confiscate that nasty thing.'

As your sword descends on her, she catches the blade in her claw, snatches it out of your hand and disappears in a puff of smoke. You are alone again. Deduct 2 points from your SKILL until you can find a replacement weapon. You have no choice but to explore this vast Library on your own. Turn to **275**.

341

You grip your sword-hilt in both hands and thrust the blade downwards, blindly, near your trapped feet. You feel the tip plunge into something spongy and after a second's pause the Lithogen reacts to this assault on its tongue. You are lifted into the air as the tongue lashes wildly from side to side and you can do nothing to stop yourself being slammed against the rough walls of the ravine as the Lithogen's tongue convulses in agony. Lose 2 points of STAMINA. If you are still alive, the tongue comes to rest again – and you are still stuck to it. To escape, you will have to keep slicing into the creature's tongue and each time you do so you will be lashed against the walls of the ravine. Roll one die; the result is the number of further points of STAMINA you must lose while cutting yourself free. If you survive the attempt, you grope your way unsteadily past the unhappy Lithogen, only to find that an unearthly luminescence is growing in the shadows of the ravine: a Spectral Stalker has sensed your presence, and is beginning to materialize. Add 1 point to your TRAIL score then *Test your Trail score*. Roll three dice. If the total is less than your TRAIL score, turn to **300**. If the total is equal to, or more than, your TRAIL score, the hideous shape slowly dissolves – you have escaped detection this time, and may continue on your way. Turn to **272**.

342

You thank the Minstrel for his offer, but you politely decline it and bid him farewell. As you walk away along the road, you hear the harp begin a plaintive melody. The sound is so beautiful that you stop to listen; you turn, and find yourself being irresistibly drawn back towards the harp. The Minstrel, sword in hand, is waiting for you. 'If you're not on my side,' he says, 'you are my enemy. Come here and die.'

Somewhere in the back of your mind a small voice is telling you that you must break away, you must run into the forest and escape. You grit your teeth and try to force your legs to carry you off the road and into the shelter of the trees. Roll four dice. If the total is less than your current STAMINA, turn to 157; if the total is equal to or more than your current STAMINA, turn to 393.

343

A Silica Serpent is a dangerous adversary. Glassy scales protect its head and body, it moves very quickly, snapping at you with its fang-filled mouth and each time it attacks it squirts from its face a jet of acid that corrodes anything it touches. But if you want to pass it, you must defeat it.

SILICA SERPENT   SKILL 7   STAMINA 11

In each Attack Round, after you have resolved the combat between your sword and the Serpent's fangs, compare Attack Strengths a second time. If you win, or the scores are the same, you have avoided the jet of acid; but if you lose, you are splashed with the liquid and must lose 2 points of STAMINA. Keep a note of the number of Attack Rounds you fight. If at any time you decide to use your LUCK in combat, turn to **264**. After four Attack Rounds, if you are still alive, turn to **176**.

344

A second pair of green eyes appears, also at floor level. As your sight adjusts to the gloom, you can see that both pairs of eyes are watching you from a crack in the floorboards – or a concealed trapdoor! As you move to defend yourself, the trapdoor is thrown open and two Goblins jump into the room. 'The innkeeper said the traveller would be drugged!' hisses one. They draw sharp blades and advance towards you. You stand in a corner so that you can fight them one at a time. Your night vision is worse than theirs: temporarily reduce your SKILL by 1 point for the duration of this fight.

	SKILL	STAMINA
First GOBLIN	5	4
Second GOBLIN	6	5

If you are still alive after three Attack Rounds, turn to **239**.

345

'I have no reason to believe you,' grunts the robed Vaskind, 'but you are obviously not of this world, and perhaps you are the warrior who, according to prophecy, will come to our aid against those who oppress the Vaskind. I have expected someone rather more impressive, but perhaps you'll do. We are prevented from rising against the tyrant Globus: he has captured and imprisoned our Queen. We used to live above, on the shore, but we have been driven beneath the waves by Globus's pets, the Silica Serpents and the Black Shadows. Globus's Vitreous Citadel, which you must reach if you are to confront him, lies on the topmost tier of the world; around it is the Crystal Garden, beautiful but deadly – it is guarded by Silica Serpents, and full of dangerous blooms. Between this lowest level and the Garden is the tier that is the home of both the Silica Serpents and the Black Shadows; the Shadows are the more deadly, but beneath their Grand Tower there is a tunnel which leads straight to the Vitreous Citadel. If you are truly an enemy of Globus, this information might assist your quest.'

You thank the Vaskind. Restore 1 point of LUCK and add 2 Provisions for the food that you are given. Two Vaskind escort you to the edge of the dome and create a bubble for you to ride in; it takes you swiftly to the surface. You wade on to the beach and head for the path that zig-zags up the face of the cliff. Turn to **12**.

Cerod's strings jangle angrily as Metron places the harp in a vice on a workbench. For many minutes the Mapmaker is busy with rulers, protractors, tubes of coloured fluids and instruments with flashing lights and glowing numbers. He consults books from his library, draws a diagram of the harp and writes pages of notes. 'A well-constructed object,' Metron says, returning the harp to you. 'The strings are arranged in order of length and the lengths are determined by a strict mathematical ratio. Quite fascinating, but I cannot imagine what it is for. It measures twelve and five-eighths *dronks* from extremity to extremity and is made from *gubis* wood. The decorations serve no function and should be removed.' Cerod is silent. You pluck the strings. It sounds like an ordinary harp; it no longer has any special properties (delete it from your *Adventure Sheet*). Metron has destroyed the harp's magical powers, and you complain bitterly. Turn to **375**.

347

Grimacing with distaste, you pull at the fleshy folds of pallid fungus that cover the doorway. The stuff comes away in long strips and soon you have cleared the door. The noxious smell, you notice, seems to emanate from the mottled skin of the fungus; the flesh inside is white, looks wholesome and has a pleasant odour. You nibble a small piece: it tastes as good as it looks. You go on to eat several large pieces. The fungus *is* wholesome: restore up to 4 points of STAMINA. You continue peeling the fungus from the door and soon you uncover the latch. You pull open the door, step through it and set off along the corridor beyond. Turn to **148**.

348

You flee beneath the pointed slabs of stone that are the upper teeth of the enormous skull, and find yourself in the dark cavern of its mouth. Looking back you see the dull glow of the bony warriors' eyes: they seem to be reluctant to follow you into the mouth of their god

Glund. You breathe a sigh of relief, but you are not safe yet. As you become accustomed to the gloom, you see that the chute down which you slid is above you and out of reach, and both of the two tunnels at the back of the cavern look dark and dangerous. Your pursuers, urged on by their leader Syzuk, are advancing hesitantly behind you. You choose one of the tunnels and trust to your good fortune: *Test your Luck*. If you are Lucky, turn to **292**. If you are Unlucky, turn to **121**.

349
You jump. The Colepod's six heavy legs just miss you as the creature thunders away into the long grass. Unhurt, you pick yourself up from the ground. Turn to **41**.

350
The toys move no closer to the bed, but continue to watch you with malevolent eyes. You sit upright on the bed, determined to stay awake all night. If you have Provisions, you can eat one meal – but because of your anxious state it restores only 2 points of STAMINA. Eventually, just before dawn, you drift into sleep – and wake to find sunlight streaming into the room and on to the toys, which are of course ordinary and lifeless. Wearily you shake your head, and catch sight of the little clown in his glass sphere. You can keep him if you want to – he reminds you of the Aleph, which you decide to use to take you away from this haunted castle. Turn to **61**.

351

In the deep darkness, the sudden appearance of your light has a blinding brilliance. You are momentarily dazzled; then you see that you are in a vast cavern — and then you see the cavern's inhabitants. Thousands of Shadowlings — the young of the Black Shadows — are carpeting the rocky floor, transfixed by your light. They are somehow even more hideous than their elder kin: their limbs are tiny, so they seem to consist only of claws, flaps of black skin and heads with gaping mouths. A few still cling to your body but they are stunned by the light and easily dislodged. As soon as you move, the others scramble away and hide behind boulders, terrified by the light you are carrying. You make your way to the end of the cave, where you find two tunnels. One of them, however, appears to fall away steeply into a noisesome pit; and you take the other, which leads upwards. Turn to **258**.

352

The curved walls are featureless and the consoles of flashing lights are sealed units. The only enclosed space big enough to conceal you is a tall metal cupboard — and it is locked. You will have to try to break the lock. Roll two dice. If the total is less than, or equal to, your SKILL score, turn to **201**. If the total is higher than your SKILL score you cannot break the lock; you must either wait in this strange metallic room (turn to **96**), or adjust some switches and step back on to the platform in the hope that it will transport you elsewhere (turn to **151**).

353

This tower is small compared to some of the others, but it is still as wide as the keep of a castle, and much taller. As you struggle across the rocky ground you become aware of a commotion in the air above you; looking up, you see a swarm of flying creatures flapping towards you like black sheets tumbling out of the sky. They are Black Shadows, the inhabitants of these cylindrical towers. As they swoop closer you see that each one is a humanoid creature, with long arms, legs, ears and tail, all of which are connected by the membrane of black skin that allows it to fly. You notice, too, the malevolent red eyes, the long sharp fangs and the talons which tip all four limbs. You hasten to the base of the tower, a solid circular wall of black stone blocks. There is no entrance, not so much as an arrow-slit. You put your back to the wall and prepare to defend yourself. If you have a Hunting-Horn turn to **80**. You can try to use the Aleph to escape from this predicament – turn to **112**. Otherwise, you will have to stand and fight – turn to **178**.

354

You are standing at the foot of a sheer cliff. Behind you, in the distance, dawn is breaking behind a range of mountains and the first rays of the morning sun are shining directly into a portal hewn into the face of the cliff immediately in front of where you are standing.

Will you enter the dark doorway (turn to **149**) or explore the area at the foot of the cliff (turn to **397**)? If you would rather use the Aleph to travel elsewhere, you take the glowing sphere from your backpack and stare into it, allowing its multitude of images to surround you – turn to **234**.

355

Although the jars are all the same size and shape, they seem to be of two different sorts. Some are marked with a roughly-stencilled diagram of a human being, while others show a human figure enclosed within a square. All the jars are lidded and sealed with wax. You break open several jars and find that they all contain a clear, odourless liquid. If you want to drink some, you can cup your hands and drink either from one of the jars marked with a plain figure (turn to **128**), or from a jar marked with a figure in a square (turn to **58**). If you would rather not drink from either sort of jar, you make your way up the stairs and leave through the door (turn to **189**).

356

You put the bottle to your lips and take a mouthful of bitter liquid. Before you can spit it out, Wayland slaps you between the shoulder-blades and you swallow it. 'Wonderful stuff!' exclaims Wayland. 'See? You're dry as a bone already.' He is right: somehow, the drink has evaporated the water that had been soaked into your clothes and hair. 'Keep the bottle; there's plenty more where that came from. It's called Siccator and one swig'll keep any liquid off your person. Might come in very handy if you come across any more practical jokers like me.' If you decide to keep the bottle, remember to note it on your *Adventure Sheet*. Turn to **175**.

Your pulse pounds in your head as the pressure of the water crushes you. Fighting to stay conscious, you struggle with the straps of your backpack as the precious air trickles from your clenched lips. At last you manage to find the little bottle of Siccator, lift if to your mouth and empty the liquid down your throat. (Delete the Siccator from your *Adventure Sheet*.) Your body tingles all over; you can no longer feel the cold water against your skin. Suddenly you find yourself rushing upwards through the sea water. Siccator and water simply do not mix and the sea is ejecting you like a stomach ejecting undigested food. You crash through the waves in a fountain of spume and are spat out on to the beach. You are winded and spend several minutes recovering your breath, but otherwise you are unhurt. There is no one on the beach, and you find nothing of interest. You decide to climb the path that zig-zags up the face of the cliff. Turn to **12**.

358

The hunters exchange neither a glance nor a shout as they glide swiftly in pursuit of the scattered woodland creatures. Within a moment, they have all swept past you; within a few seconds, they are disappearing behind a thick clump of trees. The park is peaceful again, silent and apparently empty of life under a cloudless sky. You wander aimlessly for a while, but encounter no one. There seems to be no choice but to use the Aleph to leave this place. Turn to 30.

359

You try to disentangle yourself from the fray, but your opponent clings to your legs. Within seconds other Ophidians have surrounded you and you are at the centre of a circle of spear-points. You have no doubt that you are about to be killed. Then a shadow darkens the air and, as they gaze upwards, the Ophidians cower and tremble. A Spectral Stalker is forming in the air, towering above you on four fleshless legs. *Test your Trail score.* Roll three dice. If the total is equal to, or more than, your TRAIL score, turn to 114; if the total is less than your TRAIL score, turn to 300.

360

Semeion stares long and hard at the collection of objects on the table, and then shakes his head. 'It is no use,' he says, 'I can read nothing from these few signs. They are like a jumbled sentence with the most important words missing. I am sorry, but I need more signs.' You have nothing else to offer, so instead you ask Semeion if he can give you any information about Globus. Turn to **308**.

361

Even as you push her aside to force your way through the curtain, Felice begins to change, for she is a Werecat, and as you struggle with the folds of heavy cloth she rakes you with the talons that are extending from her fur-covered hands. Roll one die and halve the result (round fractions up); the result is the number of STAM-INA points that you lose. If you survive this attack, you manage to disentangle yourself from the curtain and flee across the stage. Turn to **177**.

362

As you struggle to remain upright on the swaying bridge, you rack your brains for words that might persuade the doorway to let you live. 'Please!' you shout. 'Please spare my life, I beg you, oh most bountiful, most finely-carved, most black and gleaming doorway of the Citadel!'

The doorway remains silent, but the stone slab continues to rock dangerously. At last the voice speaks again. 'That was a pretty speech,' it says, 'and I will be merciful. I will give you a chance to enter within my portal. You must answer me this riddle:

> *Archduke Gateway am I,*
> *King of the Bridge,*
> *Emperor of the Moat;*
> *How many crowns have I?'*

Will you answer:

One?	Turn to **136**
Two?	Turn to **67**
Three?	Turn to **226**

363

Cautiously, you approach the scene of the skirmish. The Minstrel and the three boar-faced soldiers are all dead. The harp appears to be beyond repair, although it sounds the occasional note and calls plaintively for help. You pick up the Minstrel's sword and feel a surge of strength rise up your arm. It is an enchanted sword, and if you keep it – remember, you can use only one weapon at a time – you may add 1 point to your SKILL when fighting with it in combat.

As you walk away into the forest, the harp rallies the last of its energy to call after you. 'Coward!' it sings. 'Traitorous dog! You could have aided me, you could have saved my life. Now I will never resume my rightful form, never again will I see the green hills of my home. A thousand curses on you, cowardly traveller: Cerod the Minstrel's dying song condemns you!' A weight seems to settle about your heart; lose 2 points of LUCK. Disconsolate, you wander into the forest and use the Aleph to transport you elsewhere. Turn to **91**.

364

Wrestling wild bulls is one of the most dangerous entertainments demonstrated at the summer fair at Neuburg, but you always thought of yourself as an expert. Grappling with a rogue Colepod is similar, but perhaps even more difficult. It is a test of strength, agility and endurance. As it charges at you, you duck aside at the last minute. The creature careers past and you leap for its neck. Locking your wrists together with your arms clenched around its neck, you allow yourself to be swept along in the Colepod's mad gallop. Roll seven dice: if the result is less than, or equal to, the sum of you SKILL and STAMINA, turn to **256**; if the result is greater than the sum of your SKILL and STAMINA, turn to **174**.

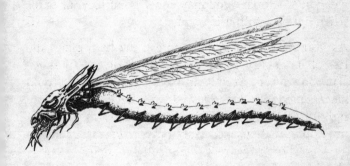

365

You gaze into the depths of the Aleph. The glowing sphere, small enough to lie cupped between your hands, seems also to be infinitely large. Uncountable swarms of visions swirl before your eyes: strange creatures, alien peoples, towns, continents, planets, stars and galaxies. Wherever you look there is an ever-changing panorama of tiny yet infinitely detailed scenes. The Aleph seems to be all around you; you are enveloped by the Aleph, and transported within it. Roll one die. If you roll an even number, turn to **51**; if an odd number, turn to **180**.

366

You close the door behind you, turn – and find yourself face to face with a creature from a nightmare! It is a patchwork monster, a living being created from assorted pieces of the bodies that Necromon begged from the Black Shadows. More horrifying than the higgledy-piggledy structure of the monster's body is the look of blank evil on its gigantic, misshapen head: no glimmer of intelligence lurks in its eyes; instead, it stares at you with a concentrated malevolence that is far worse than mere animal savagery. It drools as it tries to mouth a few words of challenge. You notice that a little pile of cheap trinkets has been arranged neatly beside the monster's otherwise jumbled bedding and possessions; perhaps it might be distracted by jewellery. If you have a Ring of Light, Drawenna's blue-gemmed ring, a Jewel of Sleep or a Seven-pointed Talisman, you may try to distract the creature – turn to **158**. If not, you will have to try to dash past – turn to **39**.

367

You trudge for what seem like endless hours along a rocky passage, until you feel weak from exhaustion. Deduct 1 point of STAMINA. You want to rest, but it seems unwise to do so in the almost complete darkness of the tunnel. At last you turn a corner to find yourself in a square courtyard with a flagstone floor. High above, you spy sunlight touching craggy rocks and dim light filters down the chimney formed by the sheer walls of the courtyard. A plume of smoke issues from a crack near the top of the shaft – but as it spirals downwards you realize that it is not smoke, but a swarm of bats! Soon they fill the courtyard, fluttering all around you and trying to bite any area of exposed flesh. You try to keep them at bay while working out how to leave the courtyard. Roll three dice. If the total is higher than your SKILL, deduct the difference between the two scores from your STAMINA. If you survive the bats' attack, you manage to see that there are four exits from the courtyard: a doorway in the middle of each wall. One has the circle and triangle symbol carved above it; you face it and decide whether to escape from the bats by going through the doorway you are facing (turn to **26**); the one behind you (turn to **206**); the one to your right (turn to **101**); or the one to your left (turn to **15**).

368

'Fate has guided your hand,' Mayrek says. 'This ball of clay is one of my most valuable possessions. It contains pure life-force, and it will perhaps save you from death one day. It will not protect you from physical harm, but if your adversaries use magical means to drain the life from your body the contents of this ball, if it is near your body, will restore you. Take it, with my thanks.'

You depart along the avenue of statues. When you are out of sight of the cave, you stop to examine the clay ball. It weighs almost nothing and seems very fragile. You shake it; it rattles. You wonder what a life-force looks like and why it rattles. If you want to crack the ball to inspect its contents, turn to **188**. If you decide to place it carefully in your backpack, record it on your *Adventure Sheet*; and then use the Aleph to leave this place – turn to **211**.

369

The tall, black-garbed Ophidians and their sinuous captive, all of them glittering like glass, are easy to follow. After leading you through steep-sided canyons and over sharp rocky ridges, they stop finally at the foot of a sheer escarpment. It is clear that the Ophidians intend to take the Silica Serpent to a cave that you can see half-way up the wall of rock. As half of the group of soldiers begin to scuttle up the rock face like huge black spiders, you see that Ophidians can climb almost as easily as they can walk. Some of the Ophidians left at the foot of the cliff begin to play haunting, discordant music on their pipes; others, with great caution, untie the Silica Serpent's wings. It seems that the music of the pipes has made the creature docile: rising into the air, it meekly follows the Ophidians who lead it up the cliff towards the cave. Soon all the Ophidians, with the Silica Serpent undulating in the air next to them, are swarming up the sheer wall of rock. Will you try to follow them (turn to **22**); or will you stay on solid ground and make your way towards the vast cliffs that

rise between this level of the Ziggurat World and the
next (turn to 4)?

370

You conceal yourself behind a bush and watch as four
excited Wood Elves emerge from a copse of trees.
They are carrying a net within which something struggles. They stop close to your hiding place, in an area
that is clear of large trees. One of them ties the net and
its still-struggling contents to a large boulder, while
another lifts his head and gives a long, loud, wavering
cry. The others scan the skies as if waiting for something
to fall from the heavens. If you decide to make yourself
known to the Wood Elves, turn to 294; if you would
rather stay hidden and continue to watch, turn to 246.

371

Struggling proves useless: the Grappler's limbs hug
you in their metallic embrace and lift you effortlessly
into the air. Sharp pincers converge on you, and you
are sure your life is about to end. The robot strips your
clothing and possessions and you are deposited, naked,
in a cage. Perhaps, at the end of this survey ship's
expedition, you will be able to convince its owners that
you are an intelligent life-form; but this adventure is
over.

372

You are too weak to survive the pressure of the light-
beam. You remain rigid, held upright by the force of
the beam, until the last breath has been squeezed from
your body and your brain ceases to function. When the

light snaps off, your lifeless body falls to the floor in the darkness.

373

You have been walking for what seems like hours, and still the corridor extends before you as far as the eye can see. As you walk, you scan the endless rows of books, and at last one attracts your attention. It is as tall as a spear and bound in fine black leather. The title, embossed in gold down the spine, is in your language: *Wizards*. Will you heave the book from its place and open it (turn to **259**)? Or are you so weary of searching this Library that you can think only of looking for a way to leave it (turn to **27**)?

374

Your well-aimed blow almost cleaves the Colepod's skull in two and the creature falls dead at your feet. You notice that there is a chain round the animal's neck, hanging from which is a small metal box, inset with a panel of glass. Upon investigation, this proves to be a lantern, presumably with magical properties, that causes a beam of light to issue from the glass panel whenever the switch on the top of the box is twisted. If you want to keep this item, note that you have a Colepod Lantern on your *Adventure Sheet*. Now turn to **170**.

375

The Mapmaker is amused at your attitude. 'You barbarians,' he chuckles, shaking his domed head, 'you're always so protective about your belongings. I expect you believe that everything you own has a lucky

charm in it. It's all mumbo-jumbo, my friend. In all my years of research I've not found a single magical item. It's all superstitious nonsense; it dissolves in the face of Science. But let me offer you something. Your home world is Titan, you say? Here, inscribed on a wooden sphere, is an exact map of your world. You may have it for only two Gold Pieces.' You are infuriated by Metron's words, but fascinated by the finely-detailed round map that he is offering to you; its size and shape are reminiscent of the Aleph. If you decide to stifle your anger and buy the map, turn to **269**. If, however, you cannot contain your rage, and attack the Map-maker, turn to **107**.

376

The ice melts surprisingly quickly. Soon rivulets of water are cascading down the sides of the block and flooding the floor. With a crash like falling masonry, a shower of ice shards erupts from the centre of the block, and the long-frozen body is free at last. A terrifying figure rises above you. Half again as tall as you, with a mottled, warty skin and a wide, frog-like face, the creature raises its huge splay-fingered hands and roars its defiant joy at finding itself freed. 'I am Baratcha, Queen of the Vaskind, ruler of the sea-people of the first level of this accursed World, and prisoner of Globus no longer — thanks to you,' she adds, looking down at you for the first time. 'What are you? Why have you come to free me?'

As quickly as you can, you explain how you come to be here, far from your home and stranded with the

Aleph on the topmost tier of Globus's strange world. Baratcha tells you that Globus himself dwells in the room beyond the dark doorway that leads from the antechamber. If you intend to confront him, she will gladly accompany you. Together you cross the ante-chamber and step through the dark doorway. Turn to **118**.

377

You pull the Aleph from your backpack and as soon as you hold the glowing sphere in your hands you are transfixed by the teeming multitude of scenes that seems to draw you ever more deeply into the Aleph's heart. Visions of bustling cities, heaving oceans and silently rotating planets surround you on all sides. You feel yourself being pulled amongst them. Roll one die. If you roll an even number, turn to **145**; if you roll an odd number, turn to **126**.

378

You step into the blue liquid. The floor of the moat slopes steeply, and you cannot prevent yourself sliding in until the liquid is up to your neck. And, of course, it is acid — a fiercely corrosive vitriol that strips your skeleton within minutes.

379

One lonely light shines in the castle's tallest tower. As you approach the chasm which separates the mountain road from the sheer crag on which the castle rises, you ensure that your footsteps are silent. But as you reach the lip of the precipice a drawbridge descends from the opposite side; candlelight flickers in the archway of the gatehouse and a voice invites you to enter. The castle is empty, its richly-furnished rooms thick with dust. You make your way to the topmost chamber and there you find the Tyrant: an aged creature, with the scaly skin of a lizard, clutching a broken staff.

'Do not fear me, Champion,' he says. 'My power is long since spent. I have been waiting here for centuries and I welcome the end of my boredom. I beg just one boon before you strike me down: show me, I pray, the means by which you came here.' The Tyrant kneels before you on creaking legs, and bows his head in submission. You take the Aleph from your pack and hold it in front of him; his eyes flash silver light. 'At last! Escape from this dreary place!' – and he lunges for the glowing sphere. Roll three dice. If the total is less than, or equal to, your SKILL, turn to **134**. If the total is greater than your SKILL score, turn to **16**.

380

This is your chance to stalk the Stalkers! Semeion's thought appears in your mind as the Telopticon's metal hoop clears to reveal the star-spangled blackness of the night sky. Something is moving against the background of pinprick lights and smudges of distant galaxies. The picture moves closer, and you can see them: several hideous shapes, almost incorporeal in the cold emptiness of space — but definitely Spectral Stalkers. There are three of them and you know that their malevolent energy is bent upon just one purpose: finding the bearer of the Aleph — you.

Notice, say Semeion's thoughts, *that they are surrounded by a halo of light — a faint glow that I imagine is visible only here in the darkness between worlds. The aura is the visible sign of the enchantment that binds them to their purpose. If we move closer, I can attempt to analyze the nature of the spell, but they will probably detect our presence. Can you afford to let them see you?* If you wish to investigate the Stalkers, turn to **227**; if, on the other hand, you decide that you cannot risk gaining any more TRAIL points, you tell Semeion that you would rather start on your travels again — turn to **23**.

381

The sound of the Horn is less strident than when you used it last, as if it had not yet recovered the strength it needs to produce its deafening clamour. Not only that: the Black Shadows seem less frightened of the noise, and merely retreat to form a circle to prevent you escaping. As the Horn's blare dies away, the Black Shadows advance again; and this time you have no choice but to fight them. Turn to **178**.

382

You should have jumped from the wagon. A Vampire is invulnerable to ordinary weapons and the Conjuror merely laughs as you strike him. The wounds that you inflict heal immediately. There is no escape: the bony fingers seize your head and pull your face to within a centimetre of the Vampire's blazing eyes. You look up for a second – and you are mesmerized. You are the Conjuror's picnic lunch as he returns home with his new bride!

383

'Such a pity,' Necromon mutters. 'I'm sure you could have been a great help to me. I insist, at any rate, that you follow the route which runs through my abode. If you step through this door, and then through the door beyond, you will find yourself on the path that leads up to the cellars of the Archmage's Vitreous Citadel. And on the way I hope you will pause to admire the weapon I am constructing to destroy Globus.' You think Necromon and step through the door through which he came earlier. Turn to **366**.

384

You uncork the bottle of Corrective Fluid and manage to dribble a little of it between Syzuk's grimacing teeth. He chokes, splutters, shakes violently and suddenly sits up with a look of astonishment in the depths of his eyes. He stares at you for a moment before gravely thanking you for saving his life; then he snatches the arrow from his shoulder as if it were no more than a splinter and jumps to his feet. 'Warriors!' he yells; and the noise of battle is suddenly stilled. 'Stop fighting! This is all a mistake. We really shouldn't spend all our time killing people. Let's go home and do something less destructive, shall we?' As one, the Skeletal Warriors turn and begin to march away from the battle! 'I don't know what was in that stuff you gave me,' says Syzuk. 'But it's made me feel like a new person. Devastation and carnage just don't have the appeal they used to. Sorry about calling off your sacrifice at such short notice. Can I give you a lift anywhere?' You decline the offer and step down from the chariot. The battlefield is already almost deserted. You take the Aleph from your pack and stare into its myriad moving pictures. It seems to expand and surround you. Roll one die: if you roll an even number, turn to **51**; if you roll an odd number, turn to **36**.

385

Step by trembling step, you approach the skeleton. It repeats its warning, but it does not move. At last you are close enough to touch it, and as your fingers close round solid bones, you laugh aloud with relief. You withdraw your hand, and see that your palm and fingers are glowing – the bones have been painted to make them shine in the dark. The skeleton is real, but it is just a lifeless collection of old bones. Its 'voice' emanates from a little machine you find lodged in its skull. Confident that you can ignore the skeleton's doom-laden warnings, you continue to edge forward into the darkness. Rounding the next corner, you fall into a chasm. Your body is broken against rocks long before you finally reach the bottom of the pit.

386

You walk steadily across the marble floor of the chamber. Suddenly a blaze of light flares in front of you, illuminating the end of the room. You see before you a vast, faceted crystal that glows with energy, a crystal that seems to be made of nothing but light itself. Standing within it is a tall figure in white robes. Powerful and imposing, the being turns towards you and you feel his eyes boring into your mind. You feel drawn towards the crystal; and for some reason, almost without noticing that you are doing it, you take the Aleph from your backpack and hold it in your outstretched hands. 'I am Globus,' says the tall figure, in a gentle voice, 'Archmage, and ruler of this world. Forgive me for greeting you from within this Prism of Power but, since I began to search for my lost bauble – which you hold there in your hands – terrible enemies have besieged me. My thanks for returning the little sphere to me. You will be richly rewarded. I know your journey has been long and perilous, but now the burden will be lifted from you. Approach, my friend, and hand the sphere to me; it will pass through the walls of the Prism if you move it slowly. Approach, and have no fear.'

If you wish to give the Aleph to Globus, turn to 338; if not, turn to 25.

387

You throw yourself at the harness of the leading war-beast, clutching at the decorations that hang from the plates of shining armour – but your grip fails and you fall to the ground beneath the flailing hooves of the tall creatures. Roll one die and lose that much STAMINA. If you are still alive, you jump to your feet as soon as the hunt has passed. *Test your Luck*. If you are Lucky, turn to **183**. If you are Unlucky, turn to **358**.

388

A swarm of black shapes, looking like hundreds of scraps of cloth, is dropping out of the sky. 'Black Shadows!' screams the Mantir leader. 'Black Shadows are coming, and the herds are unprotected. We have been distracted from our duty by this stranger. Curse Globus! His pets will feed on our Colepods – and on us if we remain unprepared! Mantirs, defend yourselves!'

The sky is alive with the flapping, flailing creatures the Mantir called Black Shadows. As they drop closer to the ground, you see that each one is in fact a humanoid creature, with long arms, legs, ears and tail, all of which are connected by the membrane of black skin that allows it to fly. You notice also the malevolent red eyes, the long sharp fangs, and the talons at the end of all four limbs. The Mantirs are huddled together face-down on the ground, spears and spiked tails thrust into the air. The Black Shadows are swooping closer; will you run from them (turn to **252**), or stand and fight (turn to **120**)? If you have a Hunting-Horn, you may blow it by turning to **309**.

389

The Grappler is the robot that is in charge of this survey's ship's wildlife collection. As far as it is concerned, you are an escaped animal and must be recaptured. Manoeuvring swiftly on its moving tracks, it blocks your attempts to sidestep and, extending its telescopic limbs, it closes in on you.

The Grappler has 10 points of SKILL. You fight it in the normal way, except that whenever it succeeds in hitting you, it does not affect your STAMINA; instead, it wraps a metal tentacle around you, reducing your SKILL by 2 points. Whenever you succeed in hitting it, roll a die: if you roll a 5 or a 6, you have managed to strike near a vital electronic circuit, and the Grappler's SKILL is reduced by 3 points. If you succeed in reducing the Grappler's SKILL to zero, turn to **55**; if the Grappler reduces your SKILL to zero, turn to **371**.

390

You draw your sword and charge into the midst of the glass flowers, striking to right and left as you run. The air is filled with the noise of splintering glass and the wailing shrieks of the flowers but there are many more blooms that remain, on all sides of you, squirting acid from within their petals. You cannot avoid being hit; the amount of damage you suffer depends entirely on the speed with which you can cut your way through the flowers. Roll three dice, and compare the total to your SKILL. If the total is greater than your SKILL, you are wounded by the flowers' corrosive spray: the difference between the two figures is the number of STAMINA points you lose. If you survive, you emerge on the other side of the flowerbed with your clothes in smoking tatters; but you are able to continue towards the Vitreous Citadel. Turn to **336**.

391

The gatehouse is undefended. The portcullis is raised and the heavy wooden doors have fallen from their hinges. You continue across a rubble-strewn courtyard and into a large hall which contains nothing but worm-eaten furniture, rotting tapestries, dust and cobwebs. And then you hear voices. You are rooted to the spot, unable to tell where the sounds are coming from. The voices are charged with emotion, shouting, sobbing and shrieking, and seem to be involved in a bitter argument about the Nursery Tower. Then all is silent again – until you hear once more the eerie scream, loud at first, then fading, and finally cut off by a distant thump. All is quiet again, but the silence is more oppressive than the noises. You turn to leave, only to find your way blocked by two figures, a man and a woman, who advance on you with outstretched arms. You cannot run back into the courtyard – will you flee into the castle (turn to **262**), or will you attack the couple (turn to **34**)?

392

You have reached the innermost chamber of the Vitreous Citadel. This was the throne room and workshop of the Archmage Globus; now, as dim lights begin to glow along the walls, you see that the room is bare. The hall is so long that, in the poor light, you cannot see the far end. You turn to the door behind you but find that it is locked, and you can see no other exit. The silence is oppressive and you sense that your long journey is about to reach its final conflict. You prepare yourself for a confrontation with Globus, but suddenly a dazzling beam of light, thrown from the far end of the hall, catches you – and holds you fast. An invisible force prevents you from moving; you can feel bands of pressure about your body, gripping you, and squeezing you more and more tightly. You cannot breathe, and the pressure increases relentlessly. If Baratcha is with you, turn to **237**; if you are alone, but have a seven-pointed Talisman, turn to **143**. Otherwise, turn to **330**.

393

You are unable to resist the call of the Ministrel's harp. On unsteady legs you stagger towards the Minstrel, but he merely smiles as he raises his sword. Your adventure ends here.

394

As your sword-blade arcs through the air, the Black Shadow releases its hold on the wall and leaps towards you. The creature screeches as your weapon slices through its membranous folds of skin, but it drops on to you and rakes you with its talons. Preparing another blow, you step back – into the empty air. For a second you stand with one foot on the stairway, arms flailing, then one final blow of the Black Shadow's claw sends you plummeting from the side of the tower to your death on the rocks below.

395

You unwrap the bundle and lift up the sphere. It is no longer shining and its moving landscapes are obscured by grey clouds. The Dragon peers at it through her spectacles, and frowns.

'Oh dear me,' she mutters. 'I really don't think that ought to be here at all. It's a very un-Limbo-like thing, if you see what I mean. I advise you to take it to our Artefacts Specialist. If anyone knows what it is, he does. His name is Wayland, and his office is a few minutes' walk along that corridor. But do be careful: he's a bit of a practical joker. I shouldn't touch the knocker on his door if I were you. Now be off with you!'

Will you follow the Dragon's pointing finger (turn to **243**), or set off in another direction to explore the corridors of the Library (turn to **275**)?

396

You advance towards the Prism, shielding your eyes from the incandescence that pulses across its facets. You press the Aleph against the surface and, after meeting some resistance, the sphere drops into the waiting hands of the Archmage. For several seconds he gazes at it in wonderment; then his face twists with scorn. 'At last you have seen reason,' he spits, 'but sadly for you it is too late. The Spectral Stalkers are here, and while under my charm they must seek and destroy the holder of the Aleph – no!!'

Globus's face is transformed into a mask of terror as he realizes that *he* is now the bearer of the Aleph. You look up and freeze in horror as the four monstrous demons lurch and spring towards the Prism. You back away, but the nightmarish creatures pay no attention to you. Their glittering eyes are fixed on the Aleph; their wriggling tentacles are hungry only for Globus's blood. In desperation he hurls the Aleph away, but it bounces off the inside of the Prism and returns to his hands. Then towering skeletal legs shatter the bright planes of the Prism, and the Spectral Stalkers are upon him. You turn away as they snatch him into the air and begin to rend his body. When you look back, he is dead. One of the Spectral Stalkers retrieves the Aleph and places it carefully next to the Archmage's torn corpse. Then, free at last, the Spectral Stalkers fade into the air. Turn to 400.

Walking away from the cliff you find that you are not, as you first thought, at its foot. You are on a ledge, below which the cliff drops precipitously to a green valley. You can find no path leading up or down the face of the cliff, but a little way from the portal there is a large flat-topped boulder on which you sit to watch the sunrise. If you have some Provisions you can eat a meal and restore up to 4 points of STAMINA.

As the sun clears the peak of the highest of the distant mountains, its light touches the surface of the boulder — and a pattern appears, etched in the stone. It is a diagram of a maze surrounding a large central area; the maze has only one entrance, and next to it is engraved a symbol — a triangle surmounted by a circle. Above the maze is an inscription: *THE SEVEN COURTYARDS OF SEMEION CRYPTOGLYPHOS*, and below it are three rhyming verses. You assume that the portal in the cliff-face is the entrance to the maze.

The diagram and the verses are reproduced on the inside front cover of this book. If you accepted paper and pencil from Metron the Mapmaker you can make a copy of the stone diagram to take with you into the maze — in other words, you can refer to the inside front cover of this book at any time in your travels. If you have no paper and pencil, you may study the diagram now — but once you enter the maze you must not consult it again.)

Now you must decide: will you venture through the portal (turn to **149**), or will you take the Aleph from your pack and, losing yourself in its myriad images, allow it to take you elsewhere (turn to **234**)?

398

The white pawn on square *G6* accepts your decision gratefully, and makes his only available move — sideways to square *G5*. There is not a single black warrior

in a square that is directly in between any two whi[te]
warriors, so you cannot kill any of them. Now it is t[he]
turn of Burud's black warriors. They do not even bother
to consult each other: you hear a noise, and turn to see
that the black pawn on *E3* is moving to *F3*. You are in
between two black warriors; and no matter how much
you turn and turn again, your armour cannot protect
you against attack from two opposite sides. Burud wins
the game and your adventure ends here.

399

You shout until your voice is as weak and exhausted as
your limbs, but no one hears you. Your legs are shaking
uncontrollably, your arms blaze with the pain of support-
ing your body, and your fingers, completely without
feeling, refuse to obey you. It is with a feeling almost of
relief that you let go.

400

Dazed, you sit in a corner of the hallway for some time.
Then you pick up the Aleph and make your way out of
the Vitreous Citadel. Cracks are appearing in the marble
and glass; you hear echoes of thunderous crashes as
spires and domes collapse. The Crystal Garden is now a
wilderness of shattered glass. As you make the long
descent through the levels of the Ziggurat World you
find that the Silica Serpents have been reduced to
glittering, insubstantial husks and the Black Shadows
have shrivelled into dry flaps of skin. On the lowest
level of the world the Wood Elves, Mantirs and Vaskind
receive you as a conquering hero and, during several
days of feasting and rejoicing, they load you with gifts

precious gems. At last you decide that you must to return home; retreating to a secluded glade in the est, you unpack the Aleph and gaze once again into teeming depths, all the while thinking of Khul.

ou open your eyes. You are sitting in a cornfield, on a slope overlooking the red roofs and majestic castle of a small town. You instantly recognize Neuburg — you are home. Your backpack is still stuffed with jewels but the Aleph, to your disappointment, is nowhere to be seen. Perhaps it is for the best: no one has the right to possess the Aleph; it should always remain lost somewhere amongst the myriad worlds of the Macrocosmos.

FIGHTING FANTASY
The Introductory Role-playing Game

Steve Jackson

Thrilling adventures of sword and sorcery come to life in the Fighting Fantasy Gamebooks, where the reader is the hero, dicing with death and demons in search of villains, treasure or freedom. Now YOU can create your own Fighting Fantasy adventures and send your friends off on dangerous missions! In this clearly written handbook there are hints on devising combats, monsters to use, tricks and tactics, as well as two mini-adventures.

THE RIDDLING REAVER

Steve Jackson

Four Fighting Fantasy episodes to be played as separate adventures or as stages in an epic adventure, *The Riddling Reaver* is a rival worthy of the most daring adventures. His mind is inscrutable – but there is no doubt about the chaos he plans to unleash on the world. He *must* be stopped, despite the hazards of the task!

A follow-up to *Fighting Fantasy: The Introductory Role-playing Game*, it contains instructions and scenarios so that you can conjure up adventures for your friends and send them on their most dangerous and puzzling mission yet.

THE TROLLTOOTH WARS

Steve Jackson

It started with an ambush. When Balthus Dire's bloodlusting Hill Goblins mount their raid on the Strongarm caravan, little do they realize what dramatic consequences their actions will have. For that caravan carries Cunnelwort, a mystical herb from Eastern Allansia, destined for none other than the evil sorcerer, Zharradan Marr! War – between two forces well-matched for evil – is soon to ensure . . . Will Balthus Dire's chaotics or Zharradan Marr's undead prove victorious? The answer is here, in the first Fighting Fantasy novel.

DEMONSTEALER

Marc Gascoigne

It started with a burglary. Borne aloft on the back of an immense bat, a sinister thief breaks into the tower of the sorcerer Yaztromo. Guided by long-dead voices, he manages to make off with an ancient scroll whose secrets could spell doom and destruction for all Allansia!

Chadda Darkmane is soon on the trail of the thief. But as the quest grows ever longer, his nagging doubts about the power of sorcery turn into nightmares. The trail leads far beyond northern Allansia, to the Pirate Coast and the twisting alleyways of Rimon, where Darkmane's nightmares become flesh! For the thief has used the ancient scroll to summon others to help him in his sorcerous task, Demons who are not bound by the constraints of earthly forms – who feast on the human spirit.

A few brave companions accompany Darkmane, but will they be enough – and in time – to stop the thief from unlocking the final secret of Yaztromo's scroll? *Demonstealer*, the second Fighting Fantasy novel in a series that began with *The Trolltooth Wars*, holds all the answers.

Steve Jackson's
SORCERY

1. *The Shamutanti Hills*

Your search for the legendary Crown of Kings take you to the Shamutanti Hills. Alive with evil creatures, lawless wanderers and bloodthirsty monsters, the land is riddled with tricks and traps waiting for the unwary traveller. Will you be able to cross the hills safely and proceed to the second part of the adventure – or will you perish in the attempt?

2. *Kharé – Cityport of Traps*

As a warrior relying on force of arms, or a wizard trained in magic, you must brave the terror of a city built to trap the unwary. You will need all your wits about you to survive the unimaginable horrors ahead and to make sense of the clues which may lead to your success – or to your doom!

3. *The Seven Serpents*

Seven deadly and magical serpents speed ahead of you to warn the evil Archmage of your coming. Will you be able to catch them before they get there?

4. *The Crown of Kings*

At the end of your long trek, you face the unknown terrors of the Mamang Fortress. Hidden inside the keep is the Crown of Kings – the ultimate goal of the *Sorcery!* epic. But beware! For if you have not defeated the Seven Serpents your arrival has been anticipated . . .

Complete with all the magical spells you will need, each book can be played either on its own or as part of the whole epic.